HOW TO CONDUCT

SELF-ADMINISTERED

S The survey kit D

AND

THE SURVEY KIT

Purpose: The purposes of this 9-volume Kit are to enable readers to prepare and conduct surveys and become better users of survey results. Surveys are conducted to collect information by asking questions of people on the telephone, face-to-face, and by mail. The questions can be about attitudes, beliefs, and behavior as well as socioeconomic and health status. To do a good survey also means knowing how to ask questions, design the survey (research) project, sample respondents, collect reliable and valid information, and analyze and report the results. You also need to know how to plan and budget for your survey.

Users: The Kit is for students in undergraduate and graduate classes in the social and health sciences and for individuals in the public and private sectors who are responsible for conducting and using surveys. Its primary goal is to enable users to prepare surveys and collect data that are accurate and useful for primarily practical purposes. Sometimes, these practical purposes overlap the objectives of scientific research, and so survey researchers will also find the Kit useful.

Format of the Kit: All books in the series contain instructional objectives, exercises and answers, examples of surveys in use and illustrations of survey questions, guidelines for action, checklists of do's and don'ts, and annotated references.

Volumes in The Survey Kit:

1. **The Survey Handbook**
   Arlene Fink

2. **How to Ask Survey Questions**
   Arlene Fink

3. **How to Conduct Self-Administered and Mail Surveys**
   Linda B. Bourque and *Eve P. Fielder*

4. **How to Conduct Interviews by Telephone and in Person**
   James H. Frey and *Sabine Mertens Oishi*

5. **How to Design Surveys**
   Arlene Fink

6. **How to Sample in Surveys**
   Arlene Fink

7. **How to Measure Survey Reliability and Validity**
   Mark S. Litwin

8. **How to Analyze Survey Data**
   Arlene Fink

9. **How to Report on Surveys**
   Arlene Fink

THE SURVEY KIT **TSK** 3

HOW TO CONDUCT SELF-ADMINISTERED AND MAIL SURVEYS

NEW ENGLAND INSTITUTE
OF TECHNOLOGY
LEARNING RESOURCES CENTER

LINDA B. BOURQUE & EVE P. FIELDER

SAGE Publications
International Educational and Professional Publisher
Thousand Oaks   London   New Delhi

For information address:

 SAGE Publications, Inc.
2455 Teller Road
Thousand Oaks, California 91320
E-mail: order@sagepub.com

SAGE Publications Ltd.
6 Bonhill Street
London EC2A 4PU
United Kingdom

SAGE Publications India Pvt. Ltd.
M-32 Market
Greater Kailash I
New Delhi 110 048 India

Printed in the United States of America

Library of Congress Cataloging-in-Publication Data

Main entry under title:

The survey kit.
    p. cm.
   Includes bibliographical references.
   Contents: v. 1. The survey handbook / Arlene Fink — v. 2. How to ask survey questions / Arlene Fink — v. 3. How to conduct self-administered and mail surveys / Linda B. Bourque, Eve P. Fielder — v. 4. How to conduct interviews by telephone and in person / James H. Frey, Sabine Mertens Oishi — v. 5. How to design surveys / Arlene Fink — v. 6. How to sample in surveys / Arlene Fink — v. 7. How to measure survey reliability and validity / Mark S. Litwin — v. 8. How to analyze survey data / Arlene Fink — v. 9. How to report on surveys / Arlene Fink.
   ISBN 0-8039-7388-8 (pbk. : The survey kit : alk. paper)
   1. Social surveys. 2. Health surveys. I. Fink, Arlene.
HN29.S724   1995
300'.723—dc20   95-12712

This book is printed on acid-free paper.

99 10 9 8 7 6 5

Sage Production Editor: Diane S. Foster
Sage Copy Editor: Joyce Kuhn
Sage Typesetter: Janelle LeMaster

Contents

Acknowledgments

We would like to thank Arlene Fink for her invitation to participate in this series and her helpful comments on earlier drafts of this manuscript; Tonya Hays, Terry Silberman, and Elizabeth Stephenson for their assistance in finding materials used in examples; Marilyn Hart and Christopher Corey for technical assistance; and Gloria Krauss for clerical and editing assistance. We particularly want to thank Deborah Riopelle, Project Coordinator for the Workplace Assault Study, for her assistance in putting together examples from that study; Maggie Robbins of the Service Employees International Union (SEIU), Bart Deiner of SEIU Local 660, and Wilma Cadorna of SEIU Local 535 who expedited the development and administration of the Workplace Assault Study.

The respondent letter used for the college student survey came from a study conducted by Jim Sidanius and Marilynn Brewer, funded by the Russell Sage Foundation (Attitudes About Cultural Diversity Among a College Population, Grant No. RSF 879.301). Data used in examples from the Prospective Evaluation for Radial Keratotomy (PERK) Study were collected and processed with funds from the National Eye Institute (Grant Nos. EY03752 and EY03761); data used in examples from the Workplace Assault Study were collected and processed with funds from the Southern California Injury Prevention Research Center under Grant No. R49-CCR903622 from the Centers for Disease Control.

How to Conduct Self-Administered and Mail Surveys: Learning Objectives

The aim of this book is to demonstrate how to develop and administer self-administered and mail surveys. Areas covered are the kinds of self-administered questionnaires, the circumstances under which they are appropriately used, and the skills needed in designing them, estimating their cost, selecting appropriate samples, and documenting the decisions made.

The specific objectives are to:

■ Describe the types of self-administered questionnaires

■ Identify the advantages and disadvantages of self-administered questionnaires

■ Decide whether a self-administered questionnaire is appropriate for your survey question

■ Determine the content of the questionnaire

■ Develop questions for a "user-friendly" questionnaire

■ Pretest, pilot-test, and revise questions

■ Format a "user-friendly" questionnaire

■ Write advance letters and cover letters that motivate and increase response rate

- Write specifications that describe the reasons for and sources of the questions on the questionnaire and the methodology used in administering the study

- Describe how to develop and produce a sample, identify potential resources for a sample, organize the sample, determine sample sizes, and increase response rate

- Inventory materials and procedures involved in mail and self-administered surveys

- Describe follow-up procedures for nonrespondents, methods of tracking a respondent, and number and timing of follow-up attempts

- Describe how returned questionnaires are processed, edited, and coded

- Describe data entry

- Describe how records are kept

- Estimate the costs of a self-administered or mailed survey

- Estimate personnel needs for a self-administered or mailed survey

- Fully document the development and administration of the questionnaire and the data collected with it

1 Overview of Self-Administered Questionnaires

Self-administered questionnaires are one of the most frequently used methods for collecting data in research studies. Furthermore, self-administered questionnaires appear in many areas of our lives. Think, for example, of the testing strategies used in most classrooms from kindergarten through graduate school. Classroom tests are a type of self-administered questionnaire. Similarly, we fill out forms or "questionnaires" to obtain everything from a driver's license to a death certificate.

Unfortunately, this very proliferation and familiarity of self-administered "questionnaires" in a wide variety of daily life settings results in neophyte surveyors often assuming that they can develop a self-administered questionnaire literally

1

overnight and use it to collect data that will be available immediately. Like any research endeavor and the use of any procedure for collecting data, the development and administration of self-administered questionnaires takes time and thought. This book outlines the circumstances under which self-administered questionnaires provide a good or at least an adequate method for collecting information, what must be considered in designing such questionnaires, and the methods used in administering them while maximizing the collection of complete, reliable, and valid data.

Types of Self-Administered Questionnaires

A self-administered questionnaire is an instrument used to collect information from people who complete the instrument themselves. The stimulus is exclusively visual. As we noted at the outset, such instruments are not used exclusively for research purposes but can be used to collect information for a wide variety of purposes and in a wide variety of settings. To date, self-administered questionnaires have almost always been administered using paper-and-pencil techniques, but with the rapid proliferation of computers and the information superhighway it is likely that such procedures will increasingly be adapted to electronic mediums. To the extent that such developments occur, it is entirely possible that auditory stimuli could be added to the visual in soliciting information through such means in much the same way that sophisticated voice-mail systems now route telephone requests for information, service, or appointments. For the purposes of this book, however, we will stick with the traditional method by which such questionnaires have been historically administered—namely, each respondent receives a printed questionnaire, which is filled out using a pen or pencil.

There are two types of self-administered questionnaires, best described as the ends of a unidimensional continuum. At one end are questionnaires that people answer in the presence of the surveyor or other supervising personnel. At the opposite end of the continuum are questionnaires completed by the respondent outside the presence of the surveyor or other monitoring personnel.

Questionnaires sent through the mail provide the most common example of unsupervised administration. Such questionnaires—frequently called "mail questionnaires"—are the major focus of this book both because of their frequent use and because almost everything that applies to a mail questionnaire has equal applicability to self-administered questionnaires distributed through other means and administered in other environments. Before turning our attention to mail questionnaires, we briefly describe some of the different kinds of supervised or partially supervised environments in which self-administered questionnaires are distributed.

SUPERVISED ADMINISTRATION

One-to-One Supervision

In the most extreme form of group administration, the respondent is in a one-to-one situation with the surveyor and the surveyor is available to answer any questions that the respondent has about the questionnaire. This type of administration is rarely used because, as we discuss later, a major reason for using self-administered questionnaires is to reduce costs. The costs associated with one-to-one administration would more closely resemble those of telephone or personal interviewing than those of self-administration.

Nonetheless, one-to-one supervision is, on occasion, used—often within the context of a study where face-to-face interviewing provides the major method of data collection. For example, under the auspices of the National Institute for Drug Abuse (NIDA) self-administered questionnaires were developed for use in ascertaining respondents' current and historical use of drugs. The questionnaires were given to respondents as part of a face-to-face interview. Their format was such that the time taken to complete the questionnaire did not differ with current or past drug history. In other words, persons who had never used drugs took just as long to complete the questionnaire as did those who had used many drugs. Within the context of the face-to-face interview, elaborate procedures were developed to ensure that the interviewer did not see the questionnaire either while it was being completed or once it was completed. The purpose here was to maximize confidentiality, the assumption being that people generally underreport the use of drugs. At the same time, the interviewer was available to answer questions or to clarify concepts should it be necessary.

Group Administration

Far more common is the situation where questionnaires are passed out in a classroom, workplace, or other group setting. Each person is expected to complete the questionnaire without consulting other persons in the group, but the surveyor or other supervisory person is available to provide introductory instructions, answer questions, and monitor the extent to which questionnaires are completed and individual respondents communicate with each other during the period of administration. Depending on the purpose of the study, the administrator may be instructed to answer and clarify any and all questions that come up or may be instructed to defer or deflect all or most questions.

For example, when group self-administration is being used to develop a questionnaire, the surveyor will probably want to learn as much as possible about how the questionnaire "works," whether respondents understand the questions asked, whether the information requested is accessible to respondents, and whether the response categories provided are exhaustive, mutually exclusive, and readily understood. In such instances, the surveyor may invite respondents to raise questions as they move through the questionnaire, or, alternatively, the surveyor may ask the respondents to first complete the questionnaire and then solicit questions, comments, and problems as part of a general discussion following the administration of the questionnaire. In either case, the person supervising the group administration must keep careful notes of the issues raised by respondents because many of the questions and comments may necessitate changes in the questionnaire.

When, in contrast, a finalized questionnaire is being administered in a group setting, supervisory personnel often are instructed to deflect any questions or comments raised by respondents. Many of the instruments used to measure attitudes, opinions, physical health status, psychological distress, and a number of other things were developed to be administered as paper-and-pencil tests in either individual or group settings. Generally, these instruments have been developed over time and with substantial attention to establishing the validity and reliability of the measure. They also were developed to assess how a particular individual respondent compares with other groups of respondents.

When such instruments are administered, the surveyor wants to do everything possible to ensure that each respondent gets an identical stimulus and that the information obtained represents that individual's feelings, attitudes, or health status. In such cases, the administrator in a group setting will generally have a scripted set of instructions used to introduce the questionnaire. These instructions may or may not be repeated on the questionnaire itself. Included in the instructions will be a statement to the effect that there are no right or wrong answers to the questions being asked, that the purpose is to find out how this particular person feels about or experiences the topic under investigation, and, when pertinent, instructions are given on how to complete the questionnaire.

Semisupervised Administration

In group administrations, as described above, it is assumed for our purposes that everyone is in the same place—usually a room—for the duration of the administration period or at least for the beginning part of it. Everyone hears the same set of verbal instructions, and everyone's questions or comments are handled in a similar way. Self-administered questionnaires are also distributed in an almost infinite variety of semisupervised administrations. For example, questionnaires might be distributed in the waiting room of a well-baby clinic by a receptionist. In such a situation, no formal presentation of verbal instructions will be given to the potential group of respondents as a whole. Rather, the receptionist will give each respondent pertinent instructions when the questionnaire is passed out. Because personnel may change during the week and the activity level in the clinic will vary, the content and extent of instructions that a given respondent receives is also likely to vary. Respondents who arrive when the clinic is quiet may receive detailed instructions, whereas those who arrive when the patient load is heavy may receive no instructions. Clearly, the constancy of the stimulus provided in such situations, at least as indicated in instructions, has the potential to influence the validity and reliability of the data obtained. Nonetheless, someone—namely, the receptionist—is, at least titularly, available to answer questions about the questionnaire and monitor the data collection effort at some minimal level.

Questionnaires are also passed out in environments such as registration lines, auditoriums, amusement centers, and airplanes and as persons are entering or exiting a store or other site. Such questionnaires can also be considered "semisupervised" to the extent that the person who distributes and collects the questionnaires is available to answer questions or provide instructions. The amount of control the surveyor exerts in such an environment is, however, limited to the selection of who will receive a questionnaire, the ability to ensure that distributed questionnaires are completed and returned, and the consistency with which any verbal instructions beyond those printed on the hard copy of the questionnaire are, in fact, solicited by or available to respondents.

UNSUPERVISED ADMINISTRATION

To our knowledge, no statistics exist regarding the number of self-administered questionnaires that are used in research projects or how they distribute between supervised and unsupervised administration, but when people think of self-administered questionnaires within a research context, in all probability they are referring to questionnaires sent through the mail, which is the primary method by which unsupervised questionnaires are administered.

When a questionnaire is administered in a completely unsupervised administration, it is imperative that the questionnaire be completely self-sufficient, or able to "stand alone." When questionnaires are sent through the mail, no member of the research staff is available to answer questions or ensure that the correct person completes the questionnaire or, indeed, that anyone completes it. Even though the questionnaire's cover sheet can include a contact name and phone number for the potential respondent's use if clarification or information is needed, the respondent must initiate such contacts. Hence, the motivation to seek information must be high.

The remainder of this book focuses on the design of mail questionnaires because the requirement that they be able to stand alone places greater restrictions on what can be included in them and requires the surveyor to pay careful attention to how clearly the questionnaire is written and presented so as to maximize the response rate.

A summary of the advantages and disadvantages of using the aforementioned ways of administering questionnaires is provided in Example 1.1.

EXAMPLE 1.1
Four Ways of Administering
Respondent-Completed Questionnaires

Type of Administration	Advantages	Disadvantages
One-to-one	Interviewer available to answer questions Maximizes confidentiality in face-to-face interviews Provides in-depth data on the answerability of questions	Expensive
Group	Consistent instructions Simultaneous administration to all respondents Administrator can answer questions Provides some information on the answerability of questions Monitor communication between respondents Monitor completion by respondents Useful in pretesting	Not usable with general populations

Type of Administration	Advantages	Disadvantages
Semisupervised	Administrator can answer questions Efficient Some ability to monitor communication between respondent and others Some ability to monitor completion Useful in pretesting Inexpensive	Samples are frequently unrepresentative Inconsistent instructions
Unsupervised	Consistent stimulus to all respondents Possibility of more representative samples	No control over who responds No direct information on answerability of questions Questionnaire must stand alone

Advantages of Self-Administered Questionnaires

COST

The single greatest advantage of self-administered question-naires is their lower cost compared to other methods (e.g., in-person and telephone interviews). Given the same-length questionnaire and same objective, a completed questionnaire administered by mail costs approximately 50% less than one administered by telephone and 75% less than one administered by personal interview.

SAMPLE RELATED

Mail questionnaires have three sample-related advantages: geographic coverage, larger samples, and wider coverage within a sample population. Although the three are interrelated, both with each other and with issues of cost, each advantage is briefly recognized.

Geographic Coverage

Mail questionnaires allow for wider geographic coverage. This is particularly true when mail questionnaires are compared to personal or face-to-face interviewing. A questionnaire can be mailed anywhere in the world, whereas face-to-face interviews tend to be restricted to a defined geographic area or areas where trained interviewers are available, can be monitored, and are able to physically contact intended respondents. Telephone interviewing also allows for a wider geographic coverage and, for all practical intents and purposes, can be conducted anywhere within the United States from a single site, assuming that funds are available for covering long-distance charges and the population under study has access to telephones. Telephone interviewing becomes problematic, however, if a substantial number of the designated respondents reside outside the United States.

For example, we used mail questionnaires to contact both undergraduate and graduate alumni of UCLA. Although most potential respondents lived in the United States (many of them in Southern California), a certain proportion of both groups resided in other countries. Because little money was available for either study, data collection using either telephone or face-to-face interviewing techniques would have prevented any attempt to obtain information from non-U.S. residents. In contrast, sending questionnaires through the mail allowed a substantial proportion of such respondents to be contacted and yielded response rates comparable to those of the sample as a whole.

Larger Samples

The lower unit cost of a mail questionnaire combined with its ability to cover a wider geographic area with little additional cost for respondents at a distance allows surveyors to study a larger sample of persons or groups. Thus, where available funds might allow for only 100 persons within a limited geographic area to be interviewed, they may allow for questionnaires to be mailed to 400-500 persons over a much larger geographic area.

Wider Coverage Within a Sample Population

Some people are reluctant to talk with people either in person or on the phone. This reluctance to talk with strangers has increased particularly in large urban areas. For example, it may be difficult or impossible to get residents of high-security buildings to agree to be interviewed—particularly if the interview is to be conducted in the home. These same persons may, however, be willing to respond to a mail questionnaire. Similarly, some persons do not have access to telephones or are reluctant to be interviewed by telephone. Again, some percentage of these persons may be willing and able to respond to a self-administered questionnaire.

In some cases, respondents are much more willing to complete a self-administered questionnaire when it can be done at their convenience rather than having to make a commitment to an interviewer to be available at an appointed time for a specific length of time to do an interview.

IMPLEMENTATION

Mail and other self-administered questionnaires are much easier to implement than other kinds of questionnaires. First, the number of personnel needed is substantially less because interviewers and those who hire, train, and supervise them are not needed. As is discussed in Chapter 2, self-administered questionnaires are shorter and simpler in structure, so fewer personnel and less complicated procedures are required for processing data once obtained. In contrast to telephone interviewing and particularly computer-assisted telephone interviewing (CATI), minimal equipment is needed to conduct a study by mail. In the simplest case, a single person can conduct an entire mail survey from start to finish.

TIMING

Unlike almost all other methods of data collection, it can be assumed that when a questionnaire is sent through the mail all members of the sample receive it simultaneously. Thus, the potential influence of events outside or unrelated to the study that might influence a potential respondent's experiences, opinions, or attitudes are reduced and can be assumed to be equal for all recipients of the questionnaire. For example, in our study of assault in the workplace, all questionnaires were mailed on the same day and were received by all respondents within the same 2- or 3-day period. Imagine telephone interviews being conducted with the same group of respondents. It is generally not possible to conduct 1,000 telephone interviews within a 2- or 3-day period—more likely, it would take weeks or even months.

Suppose that during that period of time an employee of the Los Angeles County Health Department is assaulted on the job and this assault is prominently featured in the *Los Angeles*

Times. Clearly, persons interviewed *after* the assault are likely to have different attitudes and opinions about assault in the workplace than those interviewed *before* the assault. The questionnaire that the two groups of respondents received cannot be assumed to have had an identical impact on their responses. In contrast, had the questionnaires been mailed on the same day, they can be assumed to have created a similar stimulus for all potential respondents. That is not to say that an event cannot occur at some point during the conduct of a mailed survey; however, the "window of opportunity" is greatly lessened.

SENSITIVE TOPICS

Earlier, we discussed the use of self-administered questionnaires to collect information about drug use within the context of an interview. Many surveyors believe that people are more likely to give complete and truthful information on sensitive topics if a self-administered questionnaire rather than an interview is used. Early methodological studies tended to support this perception on the part of surveyors, but more recent studies suggest that sensitive information may be collected as effectively or with even greater accuracy through telephone and face-to-face interviews.

The reason for the variation in findings across time and studies probably relates to the overall objectives of studies, the environments in which they are conducted, the ability of interviewers to establish rapport, the extent to which respondents believe that the data provided is both anonymous and confidential, and the ways in which both the overall questionnaire and individual questions are structured. We are of the opinion that sensitive topics can be effectively studied using all kinds of questionnaires.

Disadvantages of Self-Administered Questionnaires

Mail and self-administered questionnaires have a number of disadvantages that limit or prohibit their use in many research projects. These disadvantages can be grouped under three general headings: sample related, questionnaire construction, and administration.

SAMPLE RELATED

Availability of Lists

Although self-administered questionnaires are administered to admittedly nonrepresentative convenience samples, many surveyors want to use self-administered questionnaires and particularly mail questionnaires to collect data from samples that can be considered representative of the population from which they were drawn. The ability to do this—particularly when questionnaires are sent through the mail—is dependent on having a complete and accurate list of the population. To the extent that lists are unavailable, incomplete, or inaccurate, the data obtained cannot be assumed to represent the population to which the surveyor wishes to generalize.

In the worst-case scenario, the surveyor must either resort to other methods of sample generation and data collection (e.g., random digit dialing and telephone interviewing), conduct a census to establish the population from which the sample is to be drawn, or resort to convenience sampling techniques.

Response Rates

One of the greatest and most studied disadvantages to mail questionnaires is their low response rate. When a single mailing that incorporates no incentives is made to a sample of the general community, the surveyor can probably expect no better than a 20% response rate. The use of premailings, follow-up contacts, incentives, targeted populations, and a variety of other procedures combine to increase response rates, but even in the best case, response rates for mail questionnaires will be lower than those for telephone and face-to-face interviews.

Literacy and Language

One of the reasons why response rates are poor—particularly in studies targeted at general community samples—is because persons who are illiterate or who have difficulty reading simply are unable to respond even if they want to. The rate of adult illiteracy in the United States is estimated to be 20%. Obviously, persons who are functionally illiterate will be unable to complete a self-administered questionnaire and will be missed in *any* study in which they are part of the target population.

Visual acuity of the respondent can have an effect on response. Individuals who have problems with reading, such as the elderly, the visually impaired, or the dyslexic, may find the effort required to read the questionnaire too great and may not complete and return it to the surveyor. Obviously, if the target population tends to overrepresent any of these groups, it may be wise to consider an alternative method for collecting the data.

An additional problem—particularly in large urban areas on the East and West Coast—is the wide range of languages spoken in the home. For example, in Los Angeles County, 13% of the population is linguistically isolated—meaning that they speak no English—and an additional 28% report that a language other than English is the primary or only language spoken in the home. Obviously, when target populations include substantial proportions of respondents who are non-

English speakers, self-administered questionnaires must be translated and some mechanism devised for ensuring that each respondent receives a questionnaire in the correct language. As a result, data from multiple-language populations generally cannot be adequately or accurately collected using self-administered questionnaires.

QUESTIONNAIRE CONSTRUCTION

Objective

Self-administered questionnaires can be used only when the objective of the study is clear and not complex. For example, you would not want to use a mail questionnaire if you needed to collect an entire occupational history on respondents and wanted to investigate their satisfaction with their current worksite, job, employment benefits, and co-workers, and how these factors correlated with or interacted with lifestyle.

Obviously, surveyors hope to have motivated subjects in any research study, but motivation is particularly important when self-administered questionnaires are used for data collection. In the case of the workplace assault study, we decided that mail questionnaires could be used because union representatives informed us that many of their members had expressed concern about the physical safety of the environments where they worked. Thus, we believed that the topic under study would be considered important by potential respondents and that this heightened salience of the topic would increase respondents' motivation to participate in the study and hence increase our response rate.

Format

The need for a clear and noncomplex data-collection objective has ramifications for how the questionnaire is constructed and precludes the use of many strategies typically used in designing questionnaires. Chapters 2 through 4 discuss this issue in detail, so only some of these limitations are briefly noted here.

First, self-administered questionnaires must be shorter than questionnaires administered in other ways. If the questionnaire must be shorter, then obviously the number of questions asked and topics covered is reduced.

Second, the questions on self-administered questionnaires must be closed-ended ones. Although highly motivated respondents may be willing to answer a few open-ended questions, the surveyor who writes a self-administered questionnaire dominated by open-ended questions will find that few questionnaires will be returned and that those that are returned will frequently have substantial amounts of missing or irrelevant data.

Third, the questionnaire must "stand alone." In other words, all the information that the potential respondent needs to answer the questions must be provided on the questionnaire itself, as there is no interviewer available to clarify instructions or provide additional information to eliminate confusion. The objective is to make the questionnaire as easy as possible for the respondent to complete without assistance from others. This restriction means that cue cards or other visual aids cannot be used with self-administered questionnaires. It also means that the number of possible responses to a question must be limited to a number that can be readily assimilated by respondents and from which they can reasonably select those that apply to them. Thus, the need to create exhaustive lists of mutually exclusive responses may be impossible if the list becomes excessively long. Nor is it reasonable to expect respondents to rank order large numbers of alternatives. Not only are such lists burdensome for respondents to read, assimilate, and select from, but the issue of *primacy effect* becomes relevant. By primacy effect we mean respondents' tendency to select the *first* response they come to that reflects how they feel or behave even if it is not the best or most representative response available. Once a response is selected, the respondent ignores the rest of the list and goes to the next question. The necessity that the questionnaire be totally self-explanatory is probably one of the most difficult objectives to achieve in designing self-administered questionnaires.

Fourth, as part of the objective of simplifying the task for respondents, the surveyor needs to create a questionnaire without branches or skips. In other words, every question asked in the questionnaire should contain a response category that each respondent can comfortably use to describe his or her attitudes, behavior, knowledge, or characteristics. In some instances, this means that a "not applicable" alternative must be included among the responses provided for a question or series of questions.

Order Effects

When questionnaires are administered by telephone or face-to-face interviewer, the interviewer controls the order in which the questions are asked and controls whether or not the answer alternatives are made available to respondents—either by reading aloud the alternatives or by presenting them in written form on a cue card. In a self-administered questionnaire, everything is simultaneously available to the respondent. As a result, respondents can complete sections of the questionnaire in any order they choose, can refer to other sections in providing answers, and can complete the questionnaire over a series of days or even weeks. Thus, the surveyor cannot use self-administered questionnaires when one set of questions is likely to "contaminate," "bias," or "influence" answers to another section of the questionnaire.

For example, political scientists and politicians often are interested in knowing what the members of a community perceive to be the greatest problems facing their community today. What is typically asked next in the interview is a series of questions to ascertain respondents' concern over specific problems the surveyor assumes face that community. When respondents have the ability to look ahead in an interview and see the topics the surveyor selects as problems for their community, they are more likely to respond by selecting the topics that are specifically selected out later in the interview.

Similarly, it is not possible to build validity checks into a self-administered questionnaire. If, for example, the surveyor is suspicious that respondents are more likely to underreport their age when asked "How old were you on your last birthday?" than when they are asked "When were you born?", a self-administered questionnaire would not be a good way to check the "match" between the answers given to the two questions because respondents can compare their answers and change them to be consistent, if necessary. Opportunities to change answers are significantly reduced or even eliminated when interviewers control the order in which questions are asked and have been given instructions regarding the legitimacy of letting a respondent "change" an answer to a question.

ADMINISTRATION

No Control Over Who Responds

The single biggest administrative disadvantage to mail questionnaires is the fact that once the questionnaire leaves the surveyor's office, he or she has no control over who, in fact, fills it out and whether that person "consults" with others when completing it. Thus, in the Workplace Assault Study, we had a list of persons and addresses that was provided by the union. We addressed our cover letter and envelope to one union person. Once we sent the questionnaires out, however, we had no way to be sure that the designated respondent, who was a member of the union, completed the questionnaire and, furthermore, completed it without talking about it with other members of his or her household, workplace, or social group.

We know of one study conducted many years ago where questionnaires were passed out by a receptionist in a clinic waiting room. One day, the surveyor happened to walk through the waiting room just as one waiting patient was reading the questions to the rest of the waiting patients, who were then essentially "voting" on what answer should be selected. The resultant answers essentially represented a consensus of those available in the waiting room at that time rather than the opinions or behaviors of the person completing the questionnaire. Needless to say, the surveyor quickly changed his mode of administering questionnaires to a system that allowed for greater control over the number and identity of the persons completing the questionnaire. Unfortunately, when questionnaires are mailed, the surveyor has no way of checking up on these issues and must accept completed questionnaires "on faith."

Quick Turnaround

Earlier, we said that one of the advantages of mail questionnaires is that it can be assumed that all of them were administered on the same date and that all respondents received the questionnaire on the same date. In general, this means that data collected by mail will be more quickly completed than data collected by telephone or in face-to-face interviews.

There are exceptions to this. Generally, it takes a minimum of 2 weeks after each mailing for completed questionnaires to be returned to the surveyor. To the extent that the surveyor tries to maximize a good response rate by using follow-up mailings and telephone calls, the data collection period may extend to 2 or 3 months. In contrast, it is possible to conduct a telephone survey literally "overnight" if the surveyor has the resources necessary to hire a large number of interviewers and the necessary number of telephones *and if* the surveyor is willing to sacrifice a certain representativeness of the sample obtained. If, for example, all data are collected in one night from a sample of 500 persons, it clearly means that persons not at home that night have no chance of being in the sample. Also, persons whose lines were busy at the time of the attempted call will likely not be in the sample because, unlike regular telephone surveys, little or no redialing is done.

However, for interviews about fast-breaking events such as the Oklahoma City bombing on April 19, 1995, a quick telephone survey is the only way to measure rapidly changing opinions.

Self-Administered Questionnaires by Example: Assault and Vision Studies

The remainder of this book explains and describes how self-administered questionnaires are developed and administered. Two ongoing studies are used as examples.

The questionnaire used in the first study examined the extent to which members of two locals of the Service Employees International Union (SEIU) perceived their workplace sites as safe, the incidence of physical assaults experienced while at work during the preceding year, and the incidence of threats of assault within the past month. Questionnaires were sent by mail to the homes of a stratified random sample of 1,744 potential respondents on January 17, 1995 (for more information on stratified random sampling, see **How to Design Surveys** and **How to Sample in Surveys,** Vols. 5 and 6, respectively, in this series).

The questionnaire used in the second study examined the visual functioning, satisfaction, and experiences with side effects following radial keratotomy. Radial keratotomy is a surgical procedure that reduces myopia, or nearsightedness, by making slices in the patient's cornea. The questionnaire used here was administered as part of the 10-year follow-up examination in the Prospective Evaluation of Radial Keratotomy (PERK) Study, a multisite clinical trial of the 435 respondents who entered the study. In this study, questionnaires were administered at one of the nine clinical sites by clinic coordinators (for more information on clinical trials and other survey designs, see **How to Design Surveys** and **How to Sample in Surveys,** Vols. 5 and 6, respectively, in this series).

To reflect the normal progress and problems often associated with the design of data collection instruments, we discuss what worked, what did not work, and what could have been improved in our two questionnaires. Although most of our examples are drawn from these two studies, examples are also drawn from other studies where appropriate.

2 Content of the Questionnaire

This chapter begins by describing the types of data that can be collected using a questionnaire and how decisions are made regarding whether a mail questionnaire is an appropriate means of collecting data. The remainder of the chapter focuses on developing the content of the questionnaire.

Information Included in Questionnaires and Deciding Whether a Mail Questionnaire Is Appropriate

Studies of people generally collect data in one or more of five areas: personal information about the respondents, their environment, behaviors, experiences or status, and thoughts or feelings. We also sometimes think of studies focusing on people's knowledge, attitudes, and behaviors. One of the worst things that can happen to surveyors when getting ready to analyze their data is to discover that they failed to collect an essential piece of information. The first type of data is frequently referred to as **demographic data** (see **How to Ask Survey Questions,** Vol. 2 in this series, for more information on demographic data). Demographic data include such things as gender, completed education, occupational status, ethnic or racial identification, religious affiliation, and marital status. Inexperienced surveyors often forget to collect data on one or more of these important demographic variables.

The other four types of data, alone or in combination, usually form the focus of the research question. In our study on workplace assault, people are asked about their experiences —namely, were they assaulted or threatened?—their work environment, and demographic information—namely, gender, age, and the type of job they do. We hypothesize that reports of assaults and threats will be associated with the workplace environment and possibly certain demographic characteristics.

Three kinds of information must be evaluated in assessing whether or not data can be collected by mail or self-administered questionnaire. These are the literacy level of the targeted population, the motivation level of the targeted population, and whether characteristics of the research question make it amenable to data collection using a mail questionnaire.

LITERACY

In Chapter 1, we pointed out that mail questionnaires can be used only with literate respondents who are assumed to be highly motivated about the topic being studied. We have used mail questionnaires to study undergraduate and graduate alumni of UCLA. Clearly, such respondents meet the criterion of being literate. In contrast, mail questionnaires would not be a good means of studying participants in the Women, Infants, and Children's (WIC) supplemental feeding programs. WIC participants must meet a "means test" to qualify for the program. In California in 1994, the cutoff for participation was 185% of the poverty level. This meant that the annual income for a family of four could not exceed $27,380. Because income is correlated with education, a substantial number of the women enrolled in the WIC program did not complete high school, and many must be assumed to be functionally illiterate. Thus, self-administered or mail questionnaires would not be a good way to collect information about WIC participants.

MOTIVATION

Much more difficult to determine is whether a target population is motivated to answer the questionnaire. Certainly, one indication of motivation is that a group decides it needs to find out something about itself. For example, in the study of assault in the workplace, union members expressed concern about their vulnerability to assault and sought out methods by which they could do a needs assessment.

Another indicator of motivation is the amount of loyalty that individuals have to the group being studied. Using the criterion of loyalty suggests that mail questionnaires can be more successfully administered to identifiable groups—for example, alumni of UCLA, members of a professional organization, and members of a church—than to general populations.

The strength of appeal conveyed in the cover letter of the mailing can serve to motivate compliance. Developing a cover letter is discussed in Chapter 4.

AMENABLE TO STUDY

Four characteristics of a research question make it amenable to study using a mail questionnaire. First, the topic must be "contained"—that is, it must be one that can be reasonably covered in a relatively short and focused questionnaire instrument. For example, the study has a single objective, and all the "sections" of the questionnaire interrelate and work together to achieve that objective. In the Workplace Assault Study, the focus is exclusively on that—assault in the workplace. We are not trying to find out about assaults in nonworkplace environments, nor are we trying to find out other things about the workplace—for example, whether the respondents consider their jobs boring or challenging, why they chose this particular job, or even how long they have worked at the job.

Second, self-administered questionnaires generally work best when the focus is in the present. What is the respondent doing *now*? What do they know *now*? How do they feel *now*? In the Workplace Assault Study, we are not trying to find out the respondents' employment history or how and why they selected this particular career path. Rather, we *are* asking respondents about what happened to them in the past year (e.g., were they assaulted?) or in the past month (e.g., were they threatened?). Our hope is that our respondents' concerns about vulnerability to assault will result in them being highly motivated and therefore increase their willingness to complete a questionnaire that asks them to remember events that are somewhat in the past. In other words, we are assuming that the **salience** of the topic is sufficiently motivating to overcome certain other characteristics of the study that would usually argue against using a mail questionnaire.

Third, ideally the surveyor structures the questionnaire so that everyone answers every question. This can be done in one of two ways. The better of the two that the topic studied allows creation of closed-ended response lists for *every* question, thus enabling all members of the sample to describe themselves. This is sometimes accomplished by writing a question and including what is essentially a "not applicable" category as one of the response categories. For example, in our study of vision and how people use their eyes, we *failed* to allow for such a possibility in one question. The question read as follows:

When during the day do you usually read for pleasure?

Morning 1
Afternoon 2
Evening 3

This question should have had a fourth alternative answer that read "Never read for pleasure" (coded 4). The inclusion of such a response would have allowed persons who never read for pleasure to describe themselves. The omission of such an alternative increases the risk that respondents get frustrated with the questionnaire, feel that their behavior or opinions are not sufficiently represented among the answer categories presented, and, as a result, do not complete the questionnaire or fail to return it.

Alternatively, "skips" or "branching" can be used to facilitate the questionnaire's applicability to all potential respondents, but their use must be minimized. Because assault is a "rare event," we do not expect many people in our study to say that they were assaulted within the past year, *even though many of them perceive themselves to be at risk of assault.* Consequently, branching or a "skip" instruction *must* be used in this questionnaire. The first question is therefore formatted as follows:

1. How many times have you been physically attacked or assaulted at work within the past year—that is, since October 1993?

RECORD NUMBER HERE

IF 0 ATTACKS IN PAST YEAR,
SKIP TO QUESTION 24 ON PAGE 7

Persons who had been attacked within the past year answered 22 questions that asked them to describe various things about the attack. Persons who had not been attacked—the majority of respondents—skipped over this set of questions.

Similarly, Question 24 asked about threats within the past month. Again, we did not expect many people to report threats, so these people were skipped to Question 43.

24. **Within the past month**—that is, in the past 30 days—how many times have you been physically threatened or harassed?

RECORD NUMBER HERE

IF 0 THREATS IN PAST YEAR,
SKIP TO QUESTION 43 ON PAGE 13

Those who had been threatened answered a series of questions; those who had not been threatened were skipped to questions about demographic characteristics.

In this particular study, the use of two skips or branchings appears to have worked. But note that the skip is of a single kind: A person either answers a set of questions or skips over a set of questions. Respondents are *not* asked to go to *different* sections of the questionnaire according to the answers given on a screening question. Furthermore, the number of skips included in the questionnaire was restricted to two and both were of the same kind. The general rule is this:

SKIPS SHOULD BE AVOIDED IN
SELF-ADMINISTERED QUESTIONNAIRES.

If skips *must* be used, their use should be minimal and should *not* result in multiple branching operations, with one group of respondents being directed to one part of the questionnaire, a second group directed to a second part, and a third group directed to a third part. Respondents generally will *not* follow such instructions and will be irritated by the effort expended in trying to follow them. Thus, a study of a general population's use of health services where respondents vary both in age and gender is *not* amenable to study using self-administered questionnaires because of the wide variety of types of services used and because the frequency of use by males and females and by different age groups varies substantially. Far too many skips or branching operations would be necessary to provide appropriate questions for the various subgroups in the population.

Fourth, self-administered questionnaires—and particularly mail questionnaires—should not be used in exploratory studies or when the surveyor is in the process of developing a research question and the procedures by which that question will be studied. Mail questionnaires should be used only when the surveyor has a clear idea of the research objective and the parameters of the study. During the developmental stages of a study, data should be collected in ways that maximize flexibility and the ability to pursue interesting topics that may or may not be central to the original question posed. The use of focus groups; semistructured face-to-face interviews that include a lot of open-ended questions; and the ability to probe a respondent's answer, observations, and even certain kinds of secondary data are far more productive methods of collecting data in the early stages of a research project. Once the boundaries of the research question are clearly delineated and assuming the question can be appropriately operationalized in a mail questionnaire (e.g., the sample is literate and motivated), then the decision is made about whether a mail questionnaire can be used to collect the data in the study.

Checklist: Deciding Whether to Use a Mail Questionnaire

✓ **Respondents are literate and can answer all questions.**

✓ **Respondents are motivated.**

- They want to know the information.
- They feel part of a group that has reason to want the information.

✓ **The topic is amenable to study.**

- Objective is "contained" and focused.
- Questions ask about the present rather than the past or future.
- Questions are written so that they can be answered by everyone in the sample.
- Skips or branchings are avoided.
- The study is not exploratory or in the process of being developed.

Developing the Content of the Questionnaire

Once the surveyor determines that it *is* appropriate to use a mail questionnaire to collect data, the first task is to conduct a thorough search of the relevant or related literature. This literature search has two major foci. First, it helps the surveyor refine the parameters of the data collection. What other studies have been done on this topic? How were the data collected in other studies? What was the content of other data collection instruments? How can the surveyor learn from or build on these other research efforts? In developing our study on assault in the workplace we reviewed studies on occupational injury. We found out three things:

1. Most studies on workplace injury focused on deaths that occur on the job, with particular attention to homicides.

2. Most studies completed to date used secondary data sets, such as coroners' or medical examiners' reports, death certificates, or official reports made to organizations such as the Occupational Safety and Health Administration (OSHA). Needless to say, studies based on such sources tend to concentrate on the most serious occupational injuries—those that result in death or injuries sufficient to be reported to medical or other authorities.

3. The few studies that had *not* depended on secondary data sources or focused on severe injury or death had studied injuries that occurred to staff (usually nurses, in institutional settings, usually psychiatric wards).

Knowledge of this literature and what it encompassed allowed us both to define how our study would build on or extend existent work in the area and to identify the data collection instruments that we should examine in deciding how to go about our study. Namely, our study extended earlier research by assessing the frequency with which assaults occur on the job *that never are recorded in official records* and by expanding the occupational groups studied *beyond those working in locked institutional psychiatric hospitals.* Once we had completed the literature review, we knew which studies had used questionnaires to collect data, and we knew that in most cases self-administered questionnaires had been used. We then made every effort to obtain copies of all the questionnaires *as they were actually administered to respondents.* We did *not* depend on descriptions of questionnaires as they appeared in published articles or project reports.

ADOPTING STANDARD QUESTIONNAIRE BATTERIES

Ideally, we would like to find sets of questions already developed and widely used and simply adopt those questions as written. There are multiple advantages to such a strategy, and the adoption of existent standard question batteries is particularly helpful in self-administered mail questionnaires.

First, such questionnaires are almost always closed ended. As we noted in Chapter 1, respondents are generally reluctant to answer open-ended questions in a self-administered questionnaire. Thus, the selection of possible answer categories has already been worked out and tested in prior studies. Second, instructions have been developed and tested. Third, using questions *exactly* as they were used in another study allows the data you collect to be compared to the data collected in those prior studies or to a standard population. For example, many surveyors choose to ask questions about ethnicity or race exactly as asked in the U.S. Census. This decision is not made because it is thought that the U.S. Census has the "perfect" method for asking such questions but because the surveyor wants to be able to compare his or her study sample to the 1990 population in the region. Questions 4 and 7 in Figure

2–1 show how the 1990 U.S. Census determined race and ethnicity. Using questions exactly as they were worded in the 1990 Census allows the race and ethnic distribution of the study sample to be compared to a "standard" population— namely, the U.S. Census.

In other situations, we "adopt" a question or set of questions because we want to compare respondents across samples. The Prospective Evaluation of Radial Keratotomy (PERK) Study is a clinical trial for which people volunteered because they were myopic (nearsighted) and wanted radial keratotomy, which surgically reduces myopia. Because study participants were "volunteers," we were interested in finding ways to compare these myopic volunteers to a more representative sample of myopes. A series of questions that asked people about their vision was included in RAND's Health Insurance Experiment (HIE).[1] Because the HIE was done on a more representative sample and data had been collected by self-administered questionnaire, we "replicated," or adopted, some of the vision questions exactly as used by RAND. For example,

43. During the **past 3 months,** how much pain have your eyes caused you? Would you say:

    A great deal of pain 1
    Some pain. 2
    A little pain 3
    No pain at all 4

44. During the **past 3 months,** how much have eyesight problems worried or concerned you? Would you say:

    A great deal 1
    Somewhat. 2
    A little 3
    Not at all 4

	PERSON 1	PERSON 2
Please fill one column ➡ for each person listed in Question 1a on page 1.	Last name First name Middle initial	Last name First name Middle initial

2. How is this person related to PERSON 1?
Fill ONE circle for each person.
If Other relative of person in column 1, fill circle and print exact relationship, such as mother-in-law, grandparent, son-in-law, niece, cousin, and so on.
	START in this column with the household member (or one of the members) in whose name the home is owned, being bought, or rented.
	
	If there is no such person, start in this column with any adult household member.
	
	■
		If a RELATIVE of Person 1:
		○ Husband/wife ○ Brother/sister
		○ Natural-born ○ Father/mother
		   or adopted ○ Grandchild
		   son/daughter ○ Other relative ⌐
		○ Stepson/
		   stepdaughter
		If NOT RELATED to Person 1:
		○ Roomer, boarder, ○ Unmarried
		   or foster child partner
		○ Housemate, ■ ○ Other
		   roommate nonrelative

3. Sex Fill ONE circle for each person.	○ Male ○ Female	○ Male ○ Female

4. Race
Fill ONE circle for the race that the person considers himself/herself to be.
  If Indian (Amer.), print the name of the enrolled or principal tribe. ___
 	
  If Other Asian or Pacific Islander (API), print one group, for example: Hmong, Fijian, Laotian, Thai, Tongan, Pakistani, Cambodian, and so on. ___
  If Other race, print race. ➡
	○ White
	○ Black or Negro
	○ Indian (Amer.) (Print the name of the enrolled or principal tribe.)⌐
	
	○ Eskimo
	○ Aleut Asian or Pacific Islander (API)
	○ Chinese ○ Japanese
	○ Filipino ■ ○ Asian Indian
	○ Hawaiian ○ Samoan
	○ Korean ○ Guamanian
	○ Vietnamese ○ Other API ⌐
	○ Other race (Print race) ⌐
		○ White
		○ Black or Negro
		○ Indian (Amer.) (Print the name of the enrolled or principal tribe.)⌐
		
		○ Eskimo
		○ Aleut Asian or Pacific Islander (API)
		○ Chinese ○ Japanese
		○ Filipino ■ ○ Asian Indian
		○ Hawaiian ○ Samoan
		○ Korean ○ Guamanian
		○ Vietnamese ○ Other API ⌐
		○ Other race (Print race) ⌐

5. Age and year of birth
  a. Print each person's age at last birthday. Fill in the matching circle below each box.
 	
  b. Print each person's year of birth and fill the matching circle below each box.
	a. Age **b. Year of birth**
	
	0 0 0 0 0 1 ● 8 0 0 0 0
	1 0 1 0 1 0 9 0 1 0 1 0
	2 0 2 0 2 0 2 0
	3 0 3 0 3 0 3 0
	4 0 4 0 ■ 4 0 4 0
	5 0 5 0 5 0 5 0
	6 0 6 0 6 0 6 0
	7 0 7 0 7 0 7 0
	8 0 8 0 8 0 8 0
	9 0 9 0 9 0 9 0
		a. Age **b. Year of birth**
		
		0 0 0 0 0 1 ● 8 0 0 0 0
		1 0 1 0 1 0 9 0 1 0 1 0
		2 0 2 0 2 0 2 0
		3 0 3 0 3 0 3 0
		4 0 4 0 ■ 4 0 4 0
		5 0 5 0 5 0 5 0
		6 0 6 0 6 0 6 0
		7 0 7 0 7 0 7 0
		8 0 8 0 8 0 8 0
		9 0 9 0 9 0 9 0

6. Marital status Fill ONE circle for each person.	○ Now married ○ Separated ○ Widowed ○ Never married ○ Divorced	○ Now married ○ Separated ○ Widowed ○ Never married ○ Divorced

7. Is this person of Spanish/Hispanic origin?
Fill ONE circle for each person.
 	
  If Yes, other Spanish/Hispanic, print one group. ___
	○ No (not Spanish/Hispanic)
	○ Yes, Mexican, Mexican-Am., Chicano
	○ Yes, Puerto Rican ■
	○ Yes, Cuban
	○ Yes, other Spanish/Hispanic
	  (Print one group, for example: Argentinean, Colombian, Dominican, Nicaraguan, Salvadoran, Spaniard, and so on.)⌐
		○ No (not Spanish/Hispanic)
		○ Yes, Mexican, Mexican-Am., Chicano
		○ Yes, Puerto Rican
		○ Yes, Cuban
		○ Yes, other Spanish/Hispanic
		  (Print one group, for example: Argentinean, Colombian, Dominican, Nicaraguan, Salvadoran, Spaniard, and so on.)⌐

FOR CENSUS USE ➡	○ ○ □	○ ○

Figure 2–1. 1990 U.S. Census Form

45. During the **past 3 months,** how much of the time have eyesight problems kept you from doing the kinds of things other people your age do?

> All of the time 1
> Most of the time 2
> Some of the time 3
> A little of the time 4
> None of the time 5

The inclusion of these three questions in the PERK questionnaire allowed us to compare the PERK volunteers' perceptions of their eyes to those of a more representative group of myopes. What we discovered was that PERK volunteers did *not* perceive themselves as having had more pain than RAND myopes but *did* perceive themselves as being more disabled by their vision than RAND myopes. To that extent, the PERK volunteers "differed from" a more representative group of myopes.

Existent sets of questions are also adopted exactly as developed for two other reasons. First, many questionnaires—particularly those developed in the psychological literature—are under copyright. A copyright assures the author(s) of the questionnaire that it cannot be used or changed without permission. In the PERK studies, we used the SF-36 to measure the physical and mental health status of our subjects. The SF-36 was developed over a number of years under the auspices of RAND's Health Insurance Experiment. It therefore has the second characteristic that encourages the use of questionnaires exactly as written—namely, the validity and reliability of the items have been extensively tested over time and with different sample populations.

In our opinion, the SF-36 was the best measure available for assessing the concept of health status. Furthermore, it had the advantage that most of the development work on the instrument was done within the context of self-administered questionnaires. As a result, it was particularly relevant for use in the PERK Study where subjects were asked to complete questionnaires at clinical sites. The existence of the copyright assures the author(s) of the SF-36 that we will not make changes in the instrument without informing the author(s). In some instances, royalties must be paid for copyrighted questionnaires, and in all instances, appropriate citation must be made to the person(s) who developed and tested the questions.

ADAPTING SETS OF QUESTIONS

Unfortunately, many surveyors think that it is "OK" to simply select "some" questions from an instrument. Neophyte surveyors and persons developing self-administered questionnaires are particularly prone to this problem and often fall into this trap because of their eagerness to be able to say to potential respondents that "it will only take 5 minutes to fill out this questionnaire." Occasionally, a questionnaire that obtains valid and reliable data *can* be completed in 5 minutes, but it usually means that the questions have gone through extensive development and pretesting and that the topic under study is very tightly defined and presented. It usually takes respondents more than 5 minutes to provide thoughtful and complete information.

There *are* occasions when instruments are changed or adapted for use in a questionnaire. But surveyors must be aware that *when* this is done, they can no longer reference prior psychometric testing of the instrument, nor can they make direct comparisons between their sample and those to whom the original instrument was administered.

Adaptation usually occurs for one of four reasons:

- Some instruments are too long to be used in their entirety.
- A population other than the original population is being studied.
- Instruments may need to be translated into other languages.
- Surveyors may need to expand, reorder, or otherwise elaborate on items or change the procedure by which data are collected —for instance, an item written for an in-person interview may be modified for a mail questionnaire.

If modifications are made in an instrument, pilot testing should be repeated, and the instrument's reliability and validity must be reevaluated.

For example, if after due consideration a surveyor decides to use a measure of health status, but he or she simply cannot afford the time it takes to fill out the complete health status measure, because the questionnaire being developed must operationalize multiple concepts and health status is not the major focus of the study. The surveyor should not come to this conclusion without pretesting the questionnaire and clearly demonstrating that (a) the questionnaire is too long in its original version and must be shortened and (b) health status is a concept that is *not* of primary importance to testing the research question. How does the surveyor now proceed?

The first step is to contact the author(s) of the instrument and request permission to select only certain items and ask for advice on which items might best be suited to the proposed study. If the instrument is under copyright and the surveyor learns that items cannot be selected out of the battery and used in subsets, then the surveyor must find another measure of health status. Even if the questionnaire is not under copyright, the surveyor has a responsibility to respect the advice of the author(s) of the original instrument. If it is agreed that modifications can be made, then the surveyor has a responsibility to carefully document the changes made and state the reasons for the changes and to acknowledge the source of the original questionnaire. The surveyor must also retest the validity and reliability of the questions.

EXAMPLE 2.1
Adapting the SF-36 in the PERK Study

In the PERK Study, we faced a different problem. Volunteers for the PERK Study were originally enrolled in the study in the early 1980s. Upon entry to the study they were asked to complete a questionnaire. We wanted to include a measure of health status in that questionnaire and talked to surveyors at RAND about using items from the Health Insurance Experiment's questionnaire. Because data from the HIE were being analyzed at the time, they suggested a subset of items that seemed to be "best" at that stage of their analyses. Subsequent analyses of the HIE data and other data sets ultimately resulted in the development of the SF-36 as a short form of the HIE's original measure of health status. Only some of the items in the original PERK questionnaire ended up in the SF-36.

As a result, when we designed the 10-year follow-up questionnaire for PERK patients we decided that it was necessary to incorporate *both* the complete SF-36 *and* the items not included in the final SF-36 but that had been used in PERK's baseline and subsequent questionnaires. The inclusion of both sets of items meant that we could make two sets of comparisons. First, we could compare the health status of PERK volunteers at 10 years with other, more representative samples of the U.S. population, and second, we could compare the health status of PERK volunteers at 10 years with themselves at baseline and earlier follow-up periods.

We adapted both sets of items and lengthened the self-administered questionnaire. Thus, at the analysis stage, new psychometric analyses had to be completed, and during data collection, we ran the risk of having lengthened the questionnaire either unnecessarily or detrimentally.

DESIGNING YOUR OWN QUESTIONS

We recommend that, whenever possible, questions be either adopted or adapted from other studies. We think this is particularly important in self-administered questionnaires where the surveyor wants to maximize the clarity of the questionnaire. Others have developed and tested questions that can be used to operationalize concepts important to your research question. When questions are adapted or adopted from other sources, research ethics demand that you document where you obtained the instrument and give credit to the original designer(s). The following guidelines describe what needs to be considered if you must design your own questions. Some of these guidelines should also be used in evaluating whether and how questions developed by others can be adopted or adapted for your use.

Guidelines for Deciding on the Content of the Questionnaire

■ Conduct a literature review to define the parameters of the study, learn what others have done, and learn what others recommend.

- Adopt standard questionnaires to maximize closed-ended questions, because questions and instructions have already undergone development and testing, and allow for comparison with other studies. Give proper credit to persons who developed questions, and pay royalties, if required.

- Adapt questions from other studies because either the original questionnaire is too long, the mode of administration has changed, a different population is being studied, or translations must be made. Pilot testing must be repeated and reliability and validity reassessed. Also, document the source of questions adapted and the reasons for adaptation.

- Develop questions when no existent sets of questions can be adopted or adapted for the purposes of your study.

Note

1. RAND is a nonprofit institute located in Santa Monica, California, that seeks to improve public policy through research and analysis. Begun in 1971, the Health Insurance Experiment (HIE) was one of the largest controlled experiments ever attempted. Over a 15-year period, 2,700 families were randomly enrolled in health insurance plans that ranged from free care to 95% co-insurance. The objectives of the experiment were to determine which medical services to cover and the extent of coverage, to develop techniques for measuring health incomes, and to assess quality of care and the fairness and feasibility of different cost-sharing plans.

3 "User-Friendly" Questionnaires and Response Categories

Mail questionnaires more than any other type of questionnaire must maximize "user friendliness." Areas that should be considered in designing a user-friendly questionnaire are the following:

1. The way in which questions are actually written
2. How answer categories are created
3. Minimum use of open-ended questions
4. Instructions that are both clear and sufficient
5. Every effort made to avoid projecting personal biases into the wording of questions and answer categories

Construction of Questions

SHORT-AND-SPECIFIC FORMAT

Questions must be as short as possible and specific rather than general in what they reference. The creation of short, specific questions in part necessitates following the rules developed for the construction of any kind of questionnaire—for example, being careful to avoid double-barreled questions that ask two things at once, such as "How would you rate your local police on courtesy and effectiveness?" or "How often do you see or hear from your children and grandchildren?" Another rule is avoiding long run-on sentences—examples of which follow.

When you think about the traveling you might do in the next year or so, do you think you will make arrangements to travel in the next year if you decide to go by cruise ship?

Some people like to go out to the movies; others like to rent movies on video, others like to watch movies on cable TV, and others do not like to watch movies in a theatre, on video, or on TV at all. How do you feel?

Creating short, specific questions may mean asking multiple questions rather than a single question. In the Workplace Assault Study, we needed to find out about the respondent's work environment—including the hours that he or she worked. We originally designed a question that read as follows:

When do you work? _____

RECORD HOURS WORKED

During pretesting of the questionnaire, we discovered that this question was not precise enough for a variety of reasons. Some respondents in our sample worked different work shifts, others had rotating shifts, not every respondent worked the same days of the week, and so on. In responding to this question, some respondents gave us both days of the week and hours worked, others simply gave us the time that they normally arrived at work, and others simply skipped the question apparently because they found it too vague. We revised the question into a series of questions as follows:

1. What time do you usually arrive at work?

_____ AM PM

RECORD TIME OF DAY

2. What time do you usually leave work?

_____ AM PM

RECORD TIME OF DAY

3. What days of the week do you usually work?

_____

RECORD DAYS OF THE WEEK

4. How many hours a week do you usually work?

_____

RECORD NUMBER OF HOURS/WEEK

In creating this set of questions, we did two things that we generally recommend *not* doing: The answers to these questions are all open ended, and we used the adverb "usually," which is considered a vague qualifier.

There are two reasons for creating open-ended questions in this situation. First, the answers requested of respondents were not judged as burdensome, nor did they require respondents to write down a lot of information. Second, even in self-administered questionnaires, surveyors sometimes create open-ended questions because they provide better data and take up less space. Questions 1, 2, and 4 request information that can be considered "continuous" or "interval" in nature. In the case of Questions 1 and 2, the responses can be coded using a 24-hour clock; in Question 4, responses can be entered into the data set exactly as given by the respondent.

In contrast, creating closed-ended questions that included all the possible alternative responses would be difficult and would take up a lot of space that could be better used to ask additional questions. The one possible exception is Question 3, where it might have been preferable to format it as follows:

3. What days of the week do you usually work?

                          CIRCLE ALL THAT APPLY

            Sunday 1
            Monday 2
            Tuesday. 3
            Wednesday 4
            Thursday 5
            Friday . . . . : 6
            Saturday 7

Clearly, this list of responses is exhaustive and mutually exclusive. Furthermore, it allows the respondent to circle any combination of the seven responses and, quite frankly, makes future data entry easier. However, making lists for any of the other three questions would have required far more than seven mutually exclusive alternatives. Because Question 3 was part of a set of four questions, it could be argued that it is easier for the respondent to use the same kind of answer format for all four questions rather than changing to a different strategy in the middle of the set. Nonetheless, this is a judgment call on the part of the surveyor.

The word "usually" was inserted in this set of questions because of the wide variety of work schedules and sites represented in this study. Included among others surveyed were nurses, probation officers, sheriff's department employees, employees of the department of parks and recreation, and employees of the municipal courts. Many of these employees worked a standard 40-hour week, but others worked unusual hours and shifts. Nonetheless, most respondents did have a "usual" time of starting work and a "usual" time of leaving work. Inclusion of the word "usually" allowed us to communicate to respondents that there might be variation in their work days and hours without taking up further space with this set of questions.

To summarize, the original question—although short—was not sufficiently precise. It did not give us a complete picture of the days and hours that the respondent worked. In this case, the solution was to develop multiple, more specific questions. In other cases, it may be necessary to add qualifications onto the question. An example of the latter situation occurred in the PERK Study. In a follow-up questionnaire at 6 years, respondents were asked "What proportion of the time do you wear glasses or contact lenses?" Respondents frequently reacted in two ways regarding this question: First, they wrote on the questionnaire "Do you mean when we are awake?" or some other similar comment, and second, because many respondents either did not wear lenses at all **or** only needed lenses for one eye, they either provided us with that infor- mation or simply skipped the question. Once we realized that the question did not allow some of our respondents to adequately and accurately describe themselves, we were in a position of not knowing how to interpret the data for respondents who skipped the question or who did *not* write in further information.

We attempted to clarify and correct this question in two ways when we wrote the questionnaire administered at 10 years. First, we elaborated the question to read as follows:

24. What proportion of the time that you are **awake** do you wear contact lenses in **either or both** eyes or glasses?

Second, we developed a much more elaborate set of questions that asked respondents about the extent to which and the reasons for which they wore lenses and the type of lenses worn. Thus, in this instance, we had to lengthen the question to make it sufficiently specific and precise. Obviously, when it is necessary to lengthen a question, the surveyor must be clear about *why* this is being done and take care to avoid constructing an overly long question.

CAUTIONARY USE OF VAGUE QUALIFIERS

In the preceding section, we showed an example of adding the word "usually" to a question. Surveyors generally try to avoid adverbs like "usually" when they write questions because such words mean different things to different people. For example, we could have asked Question 24 as follows:

24. When you are awake do you **usually** wear glasses or contact lenses in **either or both eyes?**

Yes 1
No................ 2

The problem with using "usually" in this instance is that, for some people, "usually" would equate with wearing glasses all or most of the time; for others, it may mean that they wear glasses less than 50% of the time when they are awake, but, in their opinion, 50% of the time is too much. In other words, "usually" works as a vague qualifier in this example and, when combined with the answer categories provided, gives us imprecise information about our respondents and particularly about those who answer "yes" to this question. Our solution here was to ask respondents about the proportion of time they wore lenses. The word "proportion" could also create difficulty for some respondents who may be unfamiliar with the word or not understand it. Because this study's sample was literate and highly educated, respondents appeared to understand the term and to have no difficulty in providing an appropriate answer.

Unless the surveyor remains vigilant, all adverbs are likely candidates for vague qualifiers. Whenever an adverb shows up in a question or in a series of response alternatives, the surveyor should carefully evaluate whether the question precisely measures the concept under study.

CAUTIONARY USE OF
ABSTRACT TERMS AND JARGON

Surveyors must be particularly careful to minimize the use of abstract terms or jargon in mail questionnaires or, when used, to carefully assess that respondents understand it. This is a caveat in all questionnaire construction, but it is particularly important in mail questionnaires where there is no interviewer available to clarify or provide a definition of the abstract term if a respondent appears confused or hesitant in answering the question that contains the term.

For example, in the PERK Study, respondents were fairly sophisticated about their vision and about ophthalmology. Thus, terms like "myopia" and "radial keratotomy" would be easily understood. If, however, questions about vision were being directed to a general sample of the population, we could not assume that respondents would understand *either* term. Instead of asking if they were myopic, we would ask them if they were nearsighted or if they had difficulty seeing things at a distance. Even in the PERK questionnaire, we never used the term "myopia"; instead, we asked respondents about their ability to see at a distance.

We had a somewhat different problem in studying assaults in the workplace. The major objective of our study was to assess the prevalence of physical assaults in the workplace; we were not interested in emotional or verbal assaults. At the same time, we could not be sure that all of our respondents would understand the word "assault." So, in introducing the series of questions about physical assault, we provided respondents with a definition of physical assault. The reason for doing this was to maximize the number of respondents who understood the question in the way that we intended it. The introduction read as follows:

> In the next set of questions we would like you to describe any physical assaults or attacks that you have experienced within the past calendar year (that is, since January 1994) while you were at work. By a physical assault or attack we mean a situation where one or more persons intentionally hit you or touched you with some part of their body or with a weapon or an object.

The data collected in both the pretest and the actual study suggested that respondents understood the term "physical assault" in the way we intended.

Far more problematic was a section of the questionnaire that asked about physical threats. We could find no formal definition of "physical threat" that is used consistently in collecting official statistics or other data. To the extent that threats have been studied, surveyors have tended to create their own definition of physical threat. After substantial discussion, we decided *not* to define the term for our respondents. Instead, we considered a secondary objective of the study as that of finding out inductively what people thought constituted a "physical threat" and whether reports and perceptions of threat varied with job category, frequency of reported threats or assaults, perceptions of the work environment, demographic factors, or other characteristics of our respondents.

In deciding not to define physical threats for our respondents we put an additional burden on them in that they had to generate their own definition. Some complained about this, and the fact that we did this may have reduced our response rate.

It also provides an example of an area of research where an interview with follow-up probes would probably work better than a mail questionnaire in finding out how people heard and used the term "physical threat." However, given that we did not have the resources for interviewing our respondents but considered this an important topic for study, we chose to keep it in the questionnaire. Of course, we could have provided our respondents with a definition of threat, but in so doing, we would likely have created a definition that was either too restrictive or too broad and which, in either case, represented our own perception of the word rather than the range of perceptions of threat represented across our respondents.

To better understand this range, we asked respondents who said they had been threatened in the past month to answer an open-ended question that asked them to describe ". . . **the most serious threat** . . .", the results of which might help us generate a definition of physical threat for use in future studies.

We considered asking *all* respondents in our study to describe what they thought the term "physical threat" meant, but we decided that that would be unnecessarily burdensome for those who had not, in their opinion, experienced recent threats. Furthermore, by restricting our request to those who reported actual threats, we felt the information we received would be more accurate. This decision does not, of course, allow for the possibility that persons who did *not* report threats have a higher threshold at which they perceive a verbal or physical action to *be* a threat. For example, Respondent A may tell us that he was threatened in the past month and describe an occasion when a frustrated client swore at him. In contrast, Respondent B, who was similarly sworn at within the past month, may not remember the incident or may not consider it a threat. Hence, he does not report being threatened and, as a result, does not subsequently describe this incident to us.

In summary, abstract terms or jargon should be avoided in mail questionnaires as much as possible. If such a term must be used, the surveyor should provide a definition of it. This is possible if a standard definition is readily available in the literature but may be impossible in new areas of study. In the latter case, a mail questionnaire may not be the best way of collecting the data, but if it must be used, the respondents must be given an opportunity to tell the surveyor how they are using the term or what they understand it to mean. A decision may also have to be made as to whether all respondents will be asked to describe how they use the term or whether only those who respond in a certain way will be asked to define the term.

EASY-TO-DIFFICULT PROGRESSION

In designing all questionnaires, we try to start with the easiest questions and proceed to more complex or sensitive questions. Even though respondents can decide to answer a mail questionnaire's items in any order they choose, this rule still holds and is possibly even more important for mail questionnaires in that the surveyor wants the first few pages of the questionnaire to look inviting and to encourage the respondent to participate in the study and answer all the questions asked.

In the 10-year follow-up for the PERK Study, we were particularly interested in the extent to which and the occasions on which respondents used glasses or contact lenses to see well. Thus, a substantial part of the questionnaire focused on this topic. Figure 3-1 shows part of the sequence of questions asked.

Notice that the first question asks whether the respondent currently wears glasses or contact lenses in either eye. We then go on to ask a general question about the *amount* of time that lenses are worn. (Remember that eventually we ask respondents for more detailed information about the actual *proportion* of time they wear their lenses.) Questions 4 through 8, which are excluded from Figure 3-1, ask further general questions about respondents' vision now and prior to having radial keratotomy.

Starting with Question 9, the questions become more complex and require more thought. Because it has been hypothesized that persons who had radial keratotomy might have to wear reading glasses sooner and for a greater number of activities than would comparably aged persons who did *not* have surgery, it was important for us to obtain detailed information about the circumstances under which respondents had to wear glasses or contact lenses to see. It was also important to find out whether or not they remembered ever being told that they might have to wear lenses for close work.

Questions 9 and 10 are more difficult than Questions 2 and 3 in that they ask respondents about use of lenses for particular activities—namely, close work and reading. But Questions 9 and 10 are significantly easier to answer than Questions 11 and 12. Question 11 requires respondents to use "retrospective

Since your last examination in the PERK Study, some patients have had a lot of changes in their lenses and the extent to which they need to wear lenses. Others have had no changes. The next set of questions asks about **your** experience with corrective lenses. (CIRCLE THE NUMBER THAT CORRESPONDS TO YOUR ANSWER.)

2. Do you currently wear glasses or contact lenses in **either** eye to improve your eyesight?

    Yes . . . . GO TO Q3 1
    No . . . . GO TO Q3 2
    No, but should wear lenses. . . . ANSWER A 3

    A. Why don't you wear lenses and why should you wear lenses?

    _____

    _____

3. Do you wear these all the time or only sometimes?

    All the time . . . . ANSWER A 1
    Only sometimes . . . . ANSWER A 2
    Do not wear lenses . . . . GO TO Q4 3

    A. What are your **main** reasons for wearing corrective lenses?

    _____

    _____

9. Did anyone in the PERK Study ever tell you that **after** you had surgery you might have to wear glasses or other lenses for **reading** and other **close work**?

    Yes 1
    No 2

10. Has that happened to you? Do you **currently** wear reading glasses or lenses for:

                        CIRCLE ALL THAT APPLY

    Left eye, ... 1
    Right eye, or 2
    Neither eye? 3

11. **Following surgery** for radial keratotomy, when did you **first** start wearing reading glasses or lenses for one or both eyes?

CIRCLE ALL THAT APPLY

First started wearing reading lenses
in my right eye in: _____/_____ 1
                YEAR   MONTH

First started wearing reading lenses
in my left eye in: _____/_____ 2
                YEAR   MONTH

Do not wear reading glasses or lenses. 3

12. Some people have reading glasses or lenses but do not need to wear them for all near tasks. Others need reading lenses for only one of their eyes. Please use the following list to describe your use of lenses for **near vision** on **each eye.**

I must use glasses or some other visual aid on my **RIGHT EYE** to:

	YES	NO
Read newspaper headlines.	1	2
Read newspaper articles.	1	2
Read telephone books	1	2
Read numbers on a microwave	1	2
Read my watch.	1	2
Read a computer screen.	1	2
Read in dim light.	1	2
Read in bright light	1	2
When my right eye is tired	1	2
Read a book in the morning when I get up.	1	2
Read a book in the evening	1	2
Thread a needle	1	2
Other	1	2
SPECIFY: _____		
I use my right eye **without** a lens for near vision.	1	2
I **never** use a lens on my right eye for near vision	1	2

(continued)

I must use glasses or some other visual aid on my **LEFT EYE** to:

	YES	NO
Read newspaper headlines	1	2
Read newspaper articles	1	2
Read telephone books	1	2
Read numbers on a microwave.	1	2
Read my watch	1	2
Read a computer screen	1	2
Read in dim light	1	2
Read in bright light.	1	2
When my left eye is tired	1	2
Read a book in the morning when I get up	1	2
Read a book in the evening	1	2
Thread a needle	1	2
Other.	1	2

SPECIFY: _____

	YES	NO
I use my left eye **without** a lens for near vision	1	2
I **never** use a lens on my left eye for near vision	1	2

Figure 3–1. Constructing and Ordering Questions From Easy to Difficult

memory"—in other words, to think back in time. If they are now wearing reading glasses, when did they start? In Question 12, respondents are provided with a list of tasks that may require the use of glasses and asked whether or not they wear lenses for this task.

Furthermore, respondents are asked to *differentiate between* their two eyes. Generally, we would not expect respondents to be able to make such detailed distinctions between their eyes without help from an interviewer. However, because these particular respondents have been enrolled in a vision study for more than 10 years, they are substantially more sophisticated about their eyes than the average person is, and so we were able to obtain this information. Yet even with this sample we began with general questions and gradually progressed to more complex ones.

LOGICAL ORDER

Questions should be asked in logical order. One common error that beginning surveyors make is to order questions according to when they think about them instead of ordering them logically. In the most extreme case, respondents may be asked to flip back and forth between topics. Figure 3-2 provides an example of this kind of error. Here we have two demographic questions (Questions 1 and 3), two questions about physical activity (Questions 2 and 5), and one question about health (Question 4). Related questions should be grouped together. In other words, Questions 1 and 3 should be in sequence and placed with other demographic questions, Questions 2 and 5 should be together and placed with other questions about physical activities, and Question 4 should be placed with other questions about health status.

Figure 3-1 also provides an example of putting questions in logical order. It makes no sense to ask respondents about the circumstances under which they wear glasses or contact lenses *before* asking them if they wear lenses at all. As we see here, questions work better when general ones are asked before more specific ones.

DEMOGRAPHIC QUESTIONS PLACEMENT

In the preceding section we advised that questions be grouped by topic area. This applies to demographic questions, which ask for information about respondents (e.g., their age, gender, employment status, income, and marital status).

The question arises as to *where* in the questionnaire they should be located. Surveyors differ on this. We are of the opinion that demographic questions should be placed at the

1. Are you currently employed at a regular job?

> Yes . . . . ANSWER A-B 1
> No . . . . GO TO Q2 2

A. What days of the week do you usually work?

_____

B. What hours do you usually work?

_____

2. About how often do you participate in sports or physical activities? Would you say:

> At least once a day. 1
> Less than once a day but several times a week 2
> 2-3 times a week 3
> Once a week 4
> Less than once a week. 5
> Never. 6

3. How old were you on your last birthday?   _____

RECORD AGE

4. In general, would you say your health is:

> Excellent. 1
> Very good 2
> Good 3
> Fair 4
> Poor. 5

5. When you participate in physical activities, about how long do you participate each time?

_____

RECORD # OF MINUTES

DO NOT PARTICIPATE 999

Figure 3-2.   Example of an Illogical and Poorly Ordered Questionnaire end of the questionnaire. We recommend this for three reasons. First, mail questionnaires are almost always preceded by an introductory letter or statement that describes the subject matter of the study and encourages respondent participation. Whether such a letter is sent in advance or included with the questionnaire itself, its purpose is to intrigue respondents and encourage their participation in the study. If the first questions in the questionnaire are demographic ones, they tend to negate the purpose of the introductory letter.

Second, many people find demographic questions boring. By beginning with boring questions, the surveyor increases the probability that respondents will become disinterested in the study and never complete the questionnaire. Finally, some demographic questions, such as age and income, are considered sensitive by respondents. To start a questionnaire with questions that respondents are reluctant to answer again reduces the probability that the questionnaire will be completed and returned to the surveyor.

Although it is true that respondents can read an entire mail questionnaire before answering any of its questions, we still believe that starting a questionnaire with easy questions that immediately engage the respondent in the topic of a study will increase response rates and reduce the amount of missing data.

Other surveyors disagree with this position and believe that demographic questions should be asked at the beginning of a questionnaire. Their reasons for this position are twofold: first, that demographic questions are easier for respondents to answer because the information sought is well known to them, and second, that those respondents who return an incomplete questionnaire tend to leave the last part of the questionnaire unanswered. Thus, by putting the demographic questions at the beginning of the instrument the surveyor maximizes getting complete demographic information about the respondent.

In our opinion, this latter argument—if operative—has more salience for face-to-face or telephone interviews, where the interviewer controls the order in which questions are asked, than it does for self-administered questionnaires, where the order in which questions are answered ultimately rests with the respondent. Also, we suspect that if respondents are not going to answer a substantial number of the questions in a questionnaire they will very likely not even return the questionnaire to the surveyor.

Checklist for Constructing Questions

✓ **Keep questions short.**

✓ **Make questions specific.**

✓ **Avoid vague qualifiers.**

✓ **Avoid abstract terms.**

✓ **Avoid jargon.**

✓ **Start with easier questions and move to more difficult ones.**

✓ **Ask questions in a logical order.**

✓ **Decide WHERE to place demographic questions and WHY you are choosing that location.**

Open- Versus Closed-Ended Questions

Items in questionnaires can be either open ended or closed ended. Questions 2, 3, 10, 11, and 12 in Figure 3-1 and Questions 1, 2, and 4 in Figure 3-2 are examples of closed-ended questions. Questions 2A, 3A, and the dates in Figure 3-1 and Questions 1A, 1B, and 5 in Figure 3-2 are examples of open-ended questions. Open-ended questions have no lists of possible answers; closed-ended questions, however, contain lists of possible answers from which respondents select the answer or answers that best represent their view or situation.

Although open-ended questions are much easier to write than closed-ended items, they generally are more difficult to answer, code, and analyze because surveyors must develop code frames or categories to organize and summarize the collected data. This process is sometimes referred to as *content analysis*. In contrast, closed-ended questions are much more difficult to design but, if designed carefully and with sufficient pretesting, result in much more efficient data collection, processing, and analysis. Instead of having to write out an answer to the question, the interviewer or respondent selects the word, phrase, or statement from the list of answers that best matches the respondent's answer.

We noted in Chapter 1 that open-ended questions do not work well in self-administered or mail questionnaires. Although the neophyte surveyor may think that an open-ended question allows respondents to express themselves in greater detail and with greater accuracy without being "forced" to put themselves into a category, in fact, respondents do not like to answer open-ended questions partly because the physical process of writing out an answer is tiring. It also requires respondents to generate their own answers without any prompting from the surveyor. In general, then, open-ended questions should be avoided or used only sparingly in mail and other self-administered questionnaires.

Note in Figures 3-1 and 3-2 that open-ended questions are asked only in situations where the amount of writing demanded of a respondent is minimal, where it was not possible for the surveyor to generate a complete list of possible responses in advance (e.g., Question 2A in Figure 3-1), and where dependent questions are used. By dependent questions we mean questions that are asked of only some respondents. For example, in Figure 3-2, only those respondents who told us they are currently employed at a regular job are asked to answer Questions 1A and 1B; unemployed respondents skip these two open-ended questions.

Construction of Response Categories

Clearly, if mail questionnaires are dominated by closed-ended questions, the task of developing the response categories for such questions is particularly important. Four issues must be considered in developing response categories:

- Response categories must be exhaustive while simultaneously not being too long.
- Response categories must be mutually exclusive and the boundaries between them easily determined by respondents.
- Response categories must be set up to allow the respondent to provide multiple answers when relevant.
- When appropriate, surveyors must provide for a "residual other" category.

Generally, the number of response categories provided for each question in a mail questionnaire must be smaller than the number provided in an interviewer-administered questionnaire. The surveyor must also remember that the number and range of responses provided are always seen by the respondent, whereas in an interviewer-administered questionnaire, responses may be provided for the interviewer to use but *not* read to the respondent.

The advantage of having respondents see the response categories is that they are less likely to be influenced by either a primacy or a latency effect. In other words, instead of tending to hear the first or the last response provided and selecting one of those at the expense of all other alternatives, the respondent is more likely to "see" the entire list of responses. In general, people recognize and retain visual cues better than they do auditory cues. So if they see the list of responses, they are more likely to select the one that best represents them rather than the one that they best or most recently recall hearing.

The disadvantage is that respondents are less likely to volunteer answers that are not on the list even if the available responses do not provide an adequate description of their behavior or feelings. If response alternatives are persistently too restrictive or too vague, respondents become frustrated by their inability to accurately describe themselves. To the extent that frustration increases, response rates decrease. Thus, it is extremely important that surveyors spend sufficient time developing and pretesting the response alternatives provided for each question in a mail questionnaire.

EASILY USED CATEGORIES

In the 10-year follow-up on the PERK Study, we wanted to find out about some of the common activities for which people use their eyes (e.g., reading, driving, and watching television). We wanted to know both the extent to which they used their eyes in such activities, whether or not the amount of time they spent in such activities had changed over the past year, and when during the day they engaged in such activities. At the same time, we did not want to ask a large number of questions about these activities. Figure 3-3 shows the series of questions that was designed.

In the next set of questions we need to find out about some of your daily activities and how you spend your time.

54. Do you currently read magazines, books, and newspapers as much as you ever did, more than you did a year ago, less than you did a year ago, or don't you read for pleasure at all?

I read for pleasure:

Much more than a year ago 1
Somewhat more than a year ago 2
About the same as a year ago.............................. 3
Somewhat less than a year ago............................. 4
Do not read for pleasure at all 5
Never read for pleasure................................... 6

55. About how often do you read for pleasure?
Several times a day....................................... 1
At least once a day 2
Less than once a day but several times a week 3
2-3 times a week... 4
Once a week 5
Less than once a week 6
Never... 7

56. When during the day do you usually read for pleasure?
Morning 1
Afternoon 2
Evening................. 3

57. When you read for pleasure, about how long do you read each time?

RECORD # OF MINUTES

DO NOT READ FOR PLEASURE 999

---

58. How often did you drive a car in the past week?

    I never drove a car 1
    I no longer drive a car 2
    I did not drive in the past week 3
    I drove 2-3 times 4
    I drove several times 5
    I drove every day 6

59. How often did you watch television in the past week?

    I never have watched television 1
    I no longer watch television 2
    I did not watch TV in the past week 3
    I watched TV 2-3 times 4
    I watched TV several times. 5
    I watched TV every day. 6

60. When, during the day, do you usually watch television?

    Morning. 1
    Afternoon 2
    Evening 3

61. When you watch television, about how long do you watch each time?

    RECORD # OF MINUTES

    NEVER WATCH TELEVISION 999

Figure 3–3. Exhaustive and Mutually Exclusive Answer Categories

Notice that neither Question 56 nor 60 provides an exhaustive list of categories. To accomplish that, we should have done two things; first, added a category that allowed for persons to state that they "never read for pleasure," and second, provided instructions that allowed for persons to circle "all that apply." Question 56 provides a good example of how vague qualifiers (which frequently are adverbs) can get a surveyor into trouble. Here, the use of the word "usually" was intended to indicate "when you mainly read for pleasure" or "when you do your major pleasure reading." Many of our respondents either circled multiple alternatives or wrote along the side of the question that they read for pleasure, for example, in both the morning and the evening.

If a self-administered or mail questionnaire contains too many questions with these kinds of problems, the average respondent eventually will get irritated and, as a result, may refuse to complete the questionnaire.

MUTUALLY EXCLUSIVE CATEGORIES

Notice that Questions 54 and 55, which ask about reading for pleasure, attempt to incorporate answers that allowed us to assess both the current frequency with which people read and the extent to which reading patterns might have changed in the past year while *simultaneously* allowing response categories that differentiated persons who no longer read for pleasure from those who never read for pleasure.

Questions 58 and 59 were similarly set up to find out about driving and watching television. Unfortunately, however, the wording of the last two alternatives in Question 54 was neither clear nor mutually exclusive. In part, the confusion resulted from the fact that the present tense and past tense of the word for "read" is spelled the same way. Had we seen the confusion during pretesting, we could have rewritten the response categories in Question 54 to be analogous to those used in 58 and 59—for example, "I no longer read for pleasure" and "I have never read for pleasure."

MULTIPLE ANSWERS

Surveyors use two techniques in making response categories more flexible and exhaustive. The first of these techniques is to set up response categories so that respondents can select more than one answer to describe themselves. In Figure 3-4, Questions 25 and 26 both allow for multiple answers to be selected. Although most physical attacks are usually committed by a single person with a single weapon, Question 25 asks respondents how many people were involved in the attack, and Question 26 provides an opportunity for respondents to describe multiple attackers in terms of the kind and variety of roles that they had relative to the respondent. Thus, if in Question 25 a respondent reported having been attacked by three persons, these three persons might be described in Question 26 as a "patient/client with whom I had worked," a "patient/client whom I did not know," and "friends/relatives of a patient/client." Similarly in Question 27, the respondent might report that both a chair and fists were used in the attack.

When provisions are made for multiple answers to be given, the data set similarly must be set up to allow for the multiple answers to be efficiently and completely coded into the data set for analysis. The easiest way to do that is to create a separate variable for each answer response provided and to set up consistent codes for whether a given response is or is not selected or circled by the respondent. In the current example (Figure 3-4), we might decide that circled responses would be coded 1 for "mentioned" and those not circled would be coded 2 for "not mentioned." The responses for Question 26 would generate 10 different variables—one for each of the possible available categories provided. Similarly, the responses for Question 27 would generate six different variables.

For the respondent described above, the codes corresponding to the 10 variables created in response to Question 26 would

22. Please describe the **most serious attack you had in the last year:**

_____

_____

23. When did this attack occur? _____ / _____ / _____
                                  MONTH   DAY   YEAR

24. What time of day did this attack occur? _____
                                             RECORD TIME OF DAY

25. Were you attacked by one person or more than one person?

> One person 1
> More than one person 2
> How many? _____

26. Who was the person(s) who attacked you?

                                           CIRCLE ALL THAT APPLY

Patient/client with whom I had worked 1
Patient/client whom I did not know. 2
Friends/relatives of a patient/client 3
Co-worker/other employee 4
Supervisor or boss. 5
Subordinate or person who works for me 6
Former employee 7
Person in legal custody 8
General public/someone "off the street". 9
Other. 10
Who? _____

be 1 for each of the variables that coordinate with "patient/ client with whom I had worked," "patient/client whom I did not know," and "friends/relatives of a patient/client" and 2 for each of the other 7 variables. For Question 27, a code of 1

27. Did the person(s) who attacked you have a weapon?

CIRCLE ALL THAT APPLY

Yes, a gun.. 1

Yes, a knife...................................... 2

Yes, an object.................................... 3

    What was the object? _____

Yes, a chair or other piece of furniture 4

They used their fists or body 5

Other 6

    Please describe: _____

Figure 3–4. Examples of Residual "Other" and Use of Multiple Response Categories

would be recorded for each of the variables that correspond to "Yes, a chair or other piece of furniture" and "They used their fists or body" and 2 for each of the variables that correspond to "Yes, a gun," "Yes, a knife," "Yes, an object," and "other."

RESIDUAL "OTHER"

Residual "other" is another technique used to increase flexibility in answer categories. Both Questions 26 and 27 in Figure 3-4 include a residual "other." We consulted the literature and used information provided by focus groups and pretests in creating the list of answer categories provided in Questions 26 and 27. In Question 26, we tried to create an exhaustive list of the different kinds of people that might attack a member of Locals 535 and 660 of the Service Employees International Union. Because a wide variety of jobs are represented by the two locals, we needed to create a list that would be as exhaustive as possible and allow for the fact that, for example, psychiatric nurses and employees of the Department of Parks and Recreation interact with different types of people and different mixes of people. A psychiatric nurse who works on a locked ward will spend a substantial part of her work time interacting with incarcerated persons. In contrast, an employee of the parks department will interact primarily with fellow workers.

In creating an exhaustive list, we did not want to create too long a list or one that was *too* detailed. For example, in Question 26, we combined "patients" with "clients." Once we had finished our pretest and felt that our list was fairly exhaustive, we could not be exactly sure, so we added a residual "other." Thus, if a person was attacked by someone we failed to include in our list of categories—for example, a member of the union staff—the respondent can circle 10, which corresponds to "other," and describe this person in the space provided.

Sometimes, respondents are unsure about which category to use. For example, if a female respondent works in the tax office and is attacked by someone who works down the hall for the courts, she may not consider the person who attacked her a "co-worker or other employee." As a result, she would not circle 4, which corresponds to "co-worker/other employee," but would circle 10 for "other" and describe the person in the space provided.

Once all the questionnaires have been returned, the surveyor must decide how to handle the residual "other" answers in data analysis. There are two choices: either move the volunteered answer into one of the existent variable categories or create a new—in this case, 11th—variable that represents this new answer to Question 26. In the two examples above, we would create a new variable for the union employee but would consider the court worker a co-worker or other employee and so would recode both as 4.

Two general rules are used in deciding whether or not a new category or variable is created from answers recorded in the residual "other" category. First, we need to determine how closely the answer given in the residual "other" category relates to answer categories already specified. In the above example, we suggest that a person who works in an office down the hall is appropriately considered a co-worker but that a union employee constitutes a "different" category of person and thus necessitates the creation of a new answer category or variable. Second, we need to examine the number of times or number of respondents that put the answer into the residual "other" answer. If, for example, we had a substantial number of respondents tell us that co-workers from offices down the hall had attacked them, we might well decide that the number of responses justifies the creation of two categories of co-workers: those who work within the same office and those who work in adjacent offices. The decision as to whether or not new categories and variables should be created is made during data entry.

In developing answer categories, the surveyor tries to minimize the use of residual "other." If more than 10% of your sample has to use this category to describe its attackers, you have probably done insufficient thinking before creating your list of answer possibilities. When large numbers of respondents have to use the residual "other" category, the surveyor will have to postcode these data if they are to be meaningful. Furthermore, when respondents find that the list of responses provided for questions consistently do *not* allow them to describe themselves accurately, they will likely do one of two things. They will arbitrarily put themselves into a category simply because it is there but not because it accurately represents them, or they will become so frustrated by the questionnaire that they neither complete it nor return it.

Checklist for
Constructing Response Categories

✓ **Avoid open-ended questions.**

✓ **Create an exhaustive list of responses.**

✓ **Keep answer alternatives short and precise.**

✓ **Create mutually exclusive answer categories.**

✓ **Decide whether respondents should be restricted to a single response or allowed to provide multiple responses.**

✓ **Consider the need for a residual "other" answer category.**

Clear and Sufficient Instructions

Instructions are important in any questionnaire, but they are particularly important in a mail questionnaire where there is no interviewer who can help the respondent understand the questions or what is to be done in completing the questionnaire. Three kinds of instructions are necessary: general, transitional, and question answering.

TEN-YEAR FOLLOW-UP QUESTIONNAIRE
Prospective Evaluation of Radial Keratotomy (PERK) Study
Psychosocial and Visual Characteristics

As part of the Prospective Evaluation of Radial Keratotomy (PERK) Study, we are interested in finding out about your current vision and some of your experiences since you were last examined in the PERK Study. This questionnaire includes questions about your current vision, your general health, your use of corrective lenses, and about any problems you might have had since we last examined you. Although we know that you may find some of the questions repetitive, please answer all of them. Questions are repeated so that we can compare your experiences and opinions now—10 years after your first surgery—with your experiences before surgery, immediately after surgery, and 6 years after surgery.

We are interested in **your** opinions, ideas, and experiences. All the information you provide is confidential and will be published **only** in summary, statistical form. You will not be identified in any way. In order to get accurate information about radial keratotomy and how it affects people's vision, we need information from **all** PERK patients. So please help us by answering the questions to the best of your ability.

Please fill out the entire questionnaire now. We have arranged for you to have enough time to finish the questionnaire before we start your vision testing. When you are **finished** with the questionnaire, **seal** the questionnaire in the attached envelope and **leave it with** the clinical coordinator for the PERK Study.

Figure 3–5. Example of Instructions Used at the Beginning of a Questionnaire

GENERAL

It is usually necessary to have some set of general instructions that introduces the questionnaire itself. Figure 3–5 shows the instructions that introduced the PERK questionnaire.

Notice that the instructions provide information about the kinds of questions that will be asked. Because respondents may find some of the questions repetitive, a brief explanation of *why* repetition occurs is given. The instructions emphasize the fact that the surveyors are interested in the respondents' opinions, ideas, and experiences. This kind of instruction is particularly important when questionnaires are being distributed within an institutional site, such as a school, health clinic, or workplace, or when respondents may consciously or unconsciously think that the answers they give will be used in providing them with access to services, jobs, or goods.

The instructions also state what the respondents are supposed to do with the questionnaire when they finish it— namely, "**seal** the questionnaire in the attached envelope and **leave it with** the clinical coordinator." This procedure was developed because of our concern that respondents might think that, because they were filling out this questionnaire in a clinic, the ophthalmologist or other health personnel might have access to the questionnaire and thus know who completed it and that this access might in some way influence their health care—especially if they said something negative about the surgery or the clinical site. Surveyors can never be completely sure that such instructions eliminate "acquiescence bias," or the need to please the surveyor, but such procedures provide a method for attempting to address and reverse such processes.

Finally, this set of instructions assures respondents that they will have sufficient time to complete the questionnaire. This was added to the instructions because we discovered that earlier questionnaires had sometimes been given to patients after dilating drops were put in their eyes, which made the questionnaires difficult for them to read, or that some patients were asked to complete questionnaires as they progressed through the various ophthalmic tests.

Some questionnaires do not demand such elaborate introductory instructions. This is particularly true if cover letters are provided with the questionnaire or if advance letters have been sent to the respondents. For example, the questionnaire for the study on workplace assault did not provide lengthy introductory instructions because both advance letters and cover letters were included in the study design.

TRANSITIONAL

The second kind of instructions are those that introduce a section or provide a transition between sections of a questionnaire. Examples are the introductory statements in Figures 3–1 and 3–2. In Figure 3–3, the instructions are primarily provided so that the respondent knows that the topic of the questions is changing. The questions that preceded this instruction asked the respondents about their experiences with radial keratotomy; now they are going to be asked about daily activities. The respondents are also told that there will be multiple questions about daily activities. Such instructions give respondents a chance to "catch their breath" and help them change the focus of their thinking.

The instructions in Figure 3–1 are more elaborate. Here, the instructions are not given simply for purposes of transition; rather, they provide a context. Respondents are told that they are going to be asked questions about their experience with corrective lenses. The instructions recognize that the lens-wearing patterns of some respondents have changed since they had surgery; others have experienced little change. The purpose here is to inform respondents that the surveyor expects to find a variety of experiences reported. The respondents are also given a brief instruction about how to answer the questions, namely, "Circle the number that corresponds to your answer."

QUESTION ANSWERING

In some cases, it is necessary to provide more elaborate instructions about filling out a questionnaire. This constitutes a third kind of instructions: those whose major purpose is to provide respondents with instructions for answering the questions. The first set of questions in the PERK Study needed this kind of instructions. Respondents were asked to read and answer 63 questions that assessed both their vision and their opinions about their vision. The answer categories were the same for all 63 questions and used a 7-point Likert-type scale. The instructions read as follows:

> The first set of questions asks about your overall vision **right now** during the past week. In answering these questions, answer in terms of your **usual** lens-wearing pattern during the past week.
>
> In answering each question, use a range from one (1) to seven (7) where "1" stands for "strongly agree" and "7" stands for "strongly disagree." If you "strongly agree" with the statement, circle 1; if you agree less strongly, circle 2, which stands for "agree pretty strongly," etc.

For some populations, the surveyor would be wise to provide a verbal interpretation of what **each** of the seven numbers stands for. In this case, we knew that this sample of respondents had successfully answered similarly formatted questions in the past, so we did not spell out what each number represented. There is a fine line between giving a respondent enough instructions and giving too many. If the surveyor is going to err, however, it is probably better to give too many instructions rather than too few.

Checklist for Writing Instructions

✓ **Decide whether general instructions will be given in a cover letter, the questionnaire, or both.**

✓ Tell respondents what the questionnaire is about, what they are asked to do, and why.

✓ Tell respondents what to do with the completed questionnaire.

✓ Identify places where transitions are needed (e.g., change of topic, context for questions that follow).

✓ Determine whether detailed instructions need to be provided for a subset of questions.

Projecting the Surveyor's Ideas Onto the Respondents

Surveyors in all substantive areas are concerned with being as objective as possible in how they develop research questions and collect data to test those questions. Because human beings conduct research, it is probably impossible to eliminate all aspects of subjectivity from a research project. The task is to minimize bias and subjectivity as much as possible. The various suggestions that we have made regarding how to (a) decide on a research question, (b) write the questions, and (c) create the response categories all have as their ultimate objective maximizing the objectivity of the data collected. In collecting data from and about people, one of the most difficult things that surveyors must do is to minimize the extent to which they project their ideas about how people behave or what they think about onto the survey respondents.

Surveyors must be particularly sensitive to this problem and vigilant when they design mail questionnaires. The *way* we ask the question, the *number* of questions asked, the *order* in which we ask them, the range and type of *response categories* we provide, and the *instructions* given all provide an opportunity for making the data come out the way *we think* the world is organized. If, for example, we are convinced that there are a lot of workplace assaults, and that they occur because there are too many handguns available and because employers provide insufficient security, we can construct a questionnaire that will tend to confirm our perceptions by ignoring many of the things we recommended doing in this chapter.

In the questionnaire we designed to study workplace assaults, we asked only about assaults or threats that happened to the respondent within a specific time period. While we were designing our questionnaire, we conducted focus groups with union members. In the focus groups, most of the members reported that they had not been attacked but that they knew someone who had been attacked or that they knew someone who knew someone else who had been attacked.

One of the simplest ways to bias the estimates of attacks that we get would be to ask respondents about the number of attacks they have heard about rather than restricting our questions to attacks that they themselves experienced. This would undoubtedly raise the number of attacks reported, but the increase would be an artificial one because it is likely that multiple respondents will have heard about the *same* attack. If both Respondent A and Respondent B tell us they know someone who was attacked and we fail to find out who that person was, when the attack occurred, and so on, we are likely to conclude that *two* attacks occurred when, in fact, both respondents may be reporting the same attack.

Similarly, because we are biased toward thinking that guns are used in most attacks, we might create answer categories for Question 27 in Figure 3–4 that simply consisted of "gun" and "other." The fact that no other kind of weapon is listed may well result in respondents overreporting the use of guns simply because it is easier to circle the number associated with "gun" than it is to fill in the blank associated with "other."

Figure 3–6 shows two of the five questions that were actually used in the Workplace Assault Study. Given the bias suggested above, there are many things that we could have done in designing these questions to maximize that the data supported our biases. First, we could have restricted our questions to simply asking about the presence of security personnel and not bothered to ask Question 31 about security features and devices other than personnel.

Second, we could have constructed the questions so that a respondent circled only one answer. Because "security personnel" is only one of eight security devices listed in response to Question 31, it is likely that the restriction to a single answer would have resulted in fewer security personnel being reported.

Third, in Question 32, we similarly could have restricted our respondents to one answer, or we could have provided fewer options. For example, we might have provided only Option 1 —"Security personnel are always present in the same place" and Option 5—"There are no security personnel at my worksite."

In this chapter, we have demonstrated just a few of the ways in which the construction of self-administered questionnaires can restrict or bias the information obtained about people. Improperly designed and tested questionnaires always present a risk. Consequently, surveyors who use questionnaires to collect data must always remain aware of what their biases are and be vigilant about developing techniques that keep those biases from creeping into their questionnaires.

31. Which of the following security features/devices are available where you work:

CIRCLE ALL THAT APPLY

Locked doors to outside of building 1
Locked office doors 2
Limited public access to work areas
(counter, locked door, or other barrier) 3
Door alarms 4
Video cameras—monitored 5
Video cameras—unmonitored 6
Electronic key cards 7
Security personnel 8
Other. 9
     Please describe: _____
No security devices. 10

32. To what extent are security personnel present at your worksite:

CIRCLE ALL THAT APPLY

Security personnel are always present in the same place 1
     Please describe where they are located:

_____

Security personnel rove/roam. 2
Security personnel are on call 3
Security personnel monitor alarms and/or video monitors . . . 4
There are no security personnel at my worksite 5

Figure 3–6. Assessing the Presence of Security Features in the Workplace

Checklist for Minimizing Bias

✓ **Be aware of what your bias is.**

✓ **Develop neutral questions.**

✓ **Ask enough questions to adequately cover the topic.**

✓ **Pay attention to the order of questions.**

✓ **Provide an exhaustive range of response categories.**

✓ **Write clear and unbiased instructions.**

✓ **Take sufficient time to develop questionnaires.**

Pretesting, Pilot-Testing, and Revising Questionnaires

The first draft of a questionnaire is never perfect and ready to administer. All questionnaires should be pretested or pilot tested.

PRETESTS

Pretests are used to test sections of a questionnaire. In some cases, pretests of mail questionnaires are conducted using interviewers or focus groups. For example, in the Workplace Assault Study, our first pretest was done in focus groups.[1] Union personnel helped us get three different groups of union members together. Each group was asked to do three things:

- Complete the questionnaire as it existed at that time
- Suggest what other items should be added to the questionnaire
- Discuss aspects of the existent questionnaire that might be changed

We mentioned earlier that one of the things that came out in the focus groups was union members' suggestion that we should ask about threats and attacks that occurred to persons other than the respondent. Although we did not adopt that suggestion, we did use some of the other suggestions that participants gave us.

We wanted to include questions that asked the respondents to describe their work location, but we were somewhat unsure about how many questions should be asked and how they should be structured. Information provided in the focus groups was particularly helpful in designing that section of the questionnaire. We also became aware of something that we did not act on at that point in the questionnaire development process but which, in retrospect, became particularly salient after we finished our pilot test. Focus group members made us aware of the fact that even though employees did not report actually having been attacked or threatened on the job, they clearly felt vulnerable to such events.

PILOT TESTS

In a pilot study, the complete questionnaire is tested using the administrative procedures that will be used in the study. In the Workplace Assault Study, the participants were to be members of two union locals. We asked each of the union locals to provide us with the names and addresses of 10 persons. We wrote a cover letter that was signed by both a union official and the senior author. The packet mailed to the 20 potential respondents contained the cover letter, the questionnaire, and a self-addressed, stamped envelope for returning the completed questionnaire to us. Two weeks later we sent a postcard to all 20 respondents. The postcard reminded people that they had been sent a questionnaire, thanked those who had already returned it, and asked those who had not to please do so (see Figure 3–7 for a copy of the postcard). The postcard included

January 24, 1995

About one week ago we sent you a questionnaire about workplace safety. Your name was randomly selected from a Local 660 membership list to participate in this survey.

If you have already returned the questionnaire, please accept our sincere thanks. If not, please do it today. Because it was sent to only a small number of Local 660 members, we very much need your questionnaire if the results are to accurately represent the opinion and experiences of Local 660 members.

If you did not receive the questionnaire, or it got misplaced, please call me at 300-855-5555 and I will get another one in the mail to you immediately.

Sincerely,

Linda Bourque, Ph.D.
UCLA School of Public Health

Figure 3–7. Example of a Follow-Up Postcard

a number to call for information. Two weeks later, or 4 weeks after the original mailing, a second complete mailing was sent to all persons from whom we had not received a questionnaire.

After all the mailings, we received 12 questionnaires, or 60% of those sent, with 6 of them being returned after the first mailing, 3 after the second mailing, and 3 after the third mailing. We considered this a good response rate *until* we realized that 9 of the 12 persons who returned questionnaires were members of one of the two locals. Thus, we had a 90% response rate for one local and only a 25% response rate for the other local. The question was, why the huge difference? It turned out that the major difference had to do with how union leaders selected persons for the pilot study.

The first local selected 20 people randomly, and we then sent questionnaires to 10 of the 20. The second local selected persons for the pilot study because the union leader knew them and knew that they were members of a committee concerned with workplace assault. Needless to say, this latter group was more aware of and concerned about workplace assault and, as a result, was more motivated to participate in the study. However, these individuals were not representative of the population of the local. Thus, our 25% response rate was probably a more realistic estimate of what we would get with the questionnaire as it was then designed.

We thought for some time about how to increase our response rate in the real study. We finally decided that we needed to do a number of different things to increase potential respondents' motivation to answer the questionnaire. The first thing we did was to talk with union leaders in the two locals. Because they were interested in the study and had, in fact, asked us to conduct it, they suggested some changes that we could make in both the questionnaire and the mailings and outlined what they could do to publicize the study.

We ended up changing the questionnaire and its administration in five ways. First, one union local had a monthly newsletter. They suggested that we publish a brief article in the issue that immediately preceded the mailing of the questionnaire. We also developed a flyer that was sent to union stewards and others to put on bulletin boards at the various work sites. Second, with the union's help, we mailed a letter to the 1,744 persons comprising our sample approximately 2 weeks before the questionnaire itself was sent (see Figure 3–8). This letter was on union letterhead and was signed by union leaders. The purpose of both activities was to raise awareness within the target population and encourage our sample to participate.

Third, again at the union's suggestion, we decided that the original cover letter was too imposing and that we needed to do three things to make it more "user friendly." First, we downplayed the topic of violence and assault in the cover letter and emphasized personal safety at work. This change in emphasis was also made in the questionnaire itself where we changed the title of the questionnaire from "Physical Assault in the Workplace" to "Personal Safety at Work." Second, we shortened the cover letter itself, shortened the sentences in it, and simplified the language (see Figures 3–9 and 3–10 for copies of the original and redesigned cover letter).

Finally, we added a flyer to the packet of materials. The flyer was designed to be eye-catching and to give the potential respondent some basic information that we hoped would increase their interest in reading the cover letter and completing the questionnaire (see Figure 3–11).

We made two changes in the questionnaire itself. First, as noted above, we de-emphasized violence and assault and emphasized workplace safety. We did this by changing the title, modifying the wording of some questions, and changing the order of the questionnaire. Originally, the questionnaire was divided into four parts and presented in the following order: questions about physical assaults experienced in the past year, questions about threats experienced in the past month, questions about the workplace, and demographic questions about the respondent.

We decided that this original order was problematic for two reasons. First, by starting with questions about assault and threat, the questionnaire emphasized violence and assault. Our pretest suggested that this topic might be too extreme for our respondents and needed to be introduced less abruptly and more gradually. Second, we realized that the majority of respondents would *not* have experienced an assault or a threat. Thus, they would be instructed to skip through the first half or two thirds of the questionnaire. In contrast, everyone in our sample had a work site to describe and, remembering back to our pretests with the focus groups, that some *felt* threatened

(text continues on page 88)

SOCIAL SERVICES

UNION

AMERICAN

FEDERATION

OF NURSES

309 SO. RAYMOND

AVENUE

PASADENA

CALIFORNIA

91105

818-796-0051

FAX 818-796-2335

January 5, 1995

Dear Member,

You have been randomly selected from our membership list of Los Angeles County employees to take part in a survey about personal safety at the workplace. Your participation in the survey is very important. When you receive the questionnaire in the mail from UCLA, please fill it out and return it as soon as possible.

Our members who work for Los Angeles County are concerned about personal safety on the job. The union has raised this issue with management in contract negotiations and by filing grievances, but with only limited success. We need to do more. The SEIU Health & Safety Department and the Injury Prevention Research Center at UCLA's School of Public Health have worked with Local 535 members to develop a questionnaire addressing these issues. The questionnaire asks about concerns regarding personal safety at work as well experiences involving fear, verbal abuse, threats, and assaults on the job. Employers will not reveal this type of information. **It has to come from you!**

The results of this study will document the extent and nature of risks that our members encounter at work. Hopefully, future projects will address policies and practices intended to improve personal safety of Local 535's Los Angeles County workers.

Please fill out the survey from UCLA as soon as you receive it in the mail! If you have any questions or concerns about the survey, please feel free to call Wilma Cadorna at Local 535 or Deborah Riopelle, M.S.P.H. at UCLA at 310-825-4053.

Thanks for your help.

Sincerely,

Jerry L. Clyde   Linda Bourque, Ph.D.
President, Social Services Chapter   UCLA School of Public Health
SEIU Local 535

Figure 3–8.   Example of an Advance Letter

SOCIAL SERVICES
UNION

AMERICAN
FEDERATION
OF NURSES

309 SO. RAYMOND
AVENUE
PASADENA
CALIFORNIA
91105
818-796-0051
FAX 818-796-2335

October 7, 1994

Dear Member,

   We need your help to stop workplace violence. Many people are worried that workplace violence has increased dramatically over the past several years. Studies have shown that homicide ranks as one of the leading causes of work-related injury deaths. However, little is really known about assaults and threats of violence in the workplace. The Service Employees International Union, AFL-CIO (Locals 660 and 535) is concerned about the violence its members may encounter on a day-to-day basis. Therefore, in cooperation with the Southern California Injury Prevention Research Center at the UCLA School of Public Health, SEIU is conducting a study of workplace violence. Results from this survey will help determine the extent and nature of threats and assaults that occur in the workplace and security measures which are already in place or which may be needed.

   We need your help. Enclosed is a copy of the questionnaire that will be used in the study. This version of the questionnaire includes questions about:

   * Your experience with workplace threats and assaults
   * Security measures at your work site
   * The type of work you do and the place where you work
   * Your opinion about the content and format of the questionnaire

   Based on your comments and suggestions, the questionnaire will be revised before a final copy is mailed out to other members of Locals 660 and 535 in Los Angeles County. Please take the time to complete the questionnaire and return it in the enclosed self-addressed stamped envelope. It would be very helpful to have your completed questionnaire returned to us by October 24, 1994. We would like to send out the final survey as soon as possible.

   <u>Your responses are confidential.</u> No names or individual information will be used or released to your employer. If you have any questions or concerns, please feel free to call Deborah Riopelle, M.S.P.H. at UCLA, (310) 825-4053 or Wilma Cadorna at Local 535 (818) 796-0051.

Sincerely,

David Bullock   Linda Bourque Ph.D.
Southern Regional Director   UCLA School of Public Health

Figure 3–9.   Example of an Original Cover Letter

Social Services

Union

American

Federation

of Nurses

309 So. Raymond

Avenue

Pasadena

California

91105

818-796-0051

Fax 818-796-2335

January 17, 1995

Dear Member,

We need your help to improve personal safety on the job for Los Angeles County employees. Little is really known about personal safety and security while at work. The Service Employees International Union, Local 535 is concerned about the risks its members may encounter on a day-to-day basis. In cooperation with the Southern California Injury Prevention Research Center (SCIPRC) at the UCLA School of Public Health, we are conducting a study of workplace safety. Results from this survey will help determine measures that could be taken to protect our members.

You have been randomly selected from the membership list of Local 535's Los Angeles County employees to participate in this survey. Only a small proportion of Los Angeles County employees has been selected to participate, so your experiences and thoughts on the subject are very important. **You will be representing many employees who are similar to yourself.**

Enclosed is a copy of the questionnaire that includes questions about:

*   **The type of work you do and the place where you work**
*   **Personal safety measures at your work site**
*   **How safe or unsafe you feel at work**
*   **Your experience with workplace threats and assaults**

Please take the time to complete the questionnaire and return it in the enclosed self-addressed stamped envelope. It would be very helpful to have your completed questionnaire returned to us by **January 25, 1995**.

<u>Your responses are confidential.</u> **No names or individual information will be used or released to your employer.** If you have any questions or concerns, please feel free to call Deborah Riopelle, M.S.P.H. at UCLA, (310) 825-4053 or Wilma Cadorna at Local 535.

Sincerely,

Jerry L. Clyde   Linda Bourque, Ph.D.
President, Social Services Chapter   UCLA School of Public Health
SEIU Local 535

Figure 3–10.   Example of a Final Cover Letter

HOW SAFE IS YOUR WORKPLACE?

DO YOU FEEL UNSAFE OR INSECURE AT WORK?

HAVE YOU OR ANY OF YOUR CO-WORKERS EVER BEEN THE VICTIM OF THREATS, ASSAULTS, OR VIOLENCE ON THE JOB?

LOCAL 660
IS WORKING TO CURB WORKPLACE VIOLENCE.

WE NEED YOUR HELP!

PLEASE TAKE A FEW MOMENTS TO COMPLETE THE ENCLOSED CONFIDENTIAL SURVEY.

WORKING TOGETHER, WE CAN MAKE OUR WORKPLACE SAFER.

Figure 3–11.   Example of a Flyer Used for Motivation

in their work site even if they had not been assaulted or threatened. Thus, there was a perception of threat even if there was no objective evidence of it.

The two reasons in combination led us to reorder the questionnaire. Respondents were first asked to describe their work site and the security of their work site. They were then asked about threats they had experienced, followed by questions on assaults experienced and ending with the demographic questions. The changes made did increase our response rates somewhat. Of the original 1,744 questionnaires mailed, 38 had incorrect addresses and were returned to us. Of the remaining 1,706, 310, or 18%, were completed and returned after the first mailing. Another 258, or 15%, were completed and returned in response to the postcard. Thus, before sending out the second complete packet, 568, or 33%, of our sample had returned completed questionnaires. Another 285 completed questionnaires were returned in response to the mailing of a second questionnaire, bringing our total response rate after three mailings to 50%. This was considered insufficient for our purposes, so we turned to telephone follow-up. An attempt was made to conduct a telephone interview with each of the remaining 853 union members who had not responded to any of the three mailings.

VALUE OF PRETESTS AND PILOT TESTS

In this instance, both a pretest and a pilot test were conducted. Both provided us with valuable information, and both convinced us to change aspects of the questionnaire and the administrative procedures. They **also** made us aware of some biases that both we and the union leaders had about this study and this population of workers. We had assumed that union members were highly motivated to answer questions about assault in the workplace and that, in their eagerness to answer such questions, they would not be threatened by the topic. In fact, two things appeared to be going on. Although some proportion of these union members was concerned about workplace safety, when the questionnaire began by asking respondents to describe actual assaults, most had none to describe, and thus their motivation to answer the questions decreased. By changing the order of the questionnaire and increasing the publicity about the study, we were able to overcome some of this resistance.

Many things can be evaluated in pretests and pilot tests. Surveyors can learn how well their questions or instructions are understood and how comprehensive the response categories are. They may learn that they need to change the sequence of questions or modify the administrative procedures. Sometimes, it is necessary to ascertain how well a language translation works. Pilot tests can also help a surveyor estimate how much the data collection will cost in time and money. In this particular study, the pilot test made us realize that we had underestimated our mailing costs and the amount of personnel time it would take to set up four mailings (an advance letter, an original questionnaire, a follow-up postcard, and a second questionnaire mailing).

Pretests and pilot tests should always be conducted prior to the actual data collection, and the results should be carefully evaluated and used in making changes to the questionnaire and the study design. Such studies should always be conducted on representative members of the intended target population and, when serious or multiple problems are identified during a pretest or pilot test, revisions should be made and pretesting continued until the surveyor is confident that the data collection instrument is effectively and efficiently obtaining the data needed to validly and reliably test the research question.

Checklist for Conducting
Pretests and Pilot Tests

✓ **Decide whether pretests, pilot tests, or both are needed.**

✓ **Decide whether multiple pretests or pilot tests will be needed.**

✓ **How will pretests be conducted—in focus groups, by interview, in group administrations, or through the mail?**

✓ **Who is the sample for a pilot test or pretest—should it be representative?**

✓ **Pay careful attention to the results of pretests and pilot tests:**

- Are questions understood?
- Are instructions clear?
- Is the order of questions appropriate?
- Are the objectives of the study clearly understood by both surveyors and respondents?
- Have costs been accurately projected?

Note

1. The use of focus groups to develop questions, item series, and/or concept areas has been increasing in recent years. A focus group usually consists of a trained moderator and 8 to 10 participants. The moderator is skilled in focus group techniques and either has some background in the topic under study or is briefed extensively on the topic. The participants are usually recruited at random from the community or may have responded to a survey in the past. If the topic area is one requiring particular knowledge or skills, recruiting will be directed exclusively toward individuals with those skills. A focus group session typically lasts 90 minutes, is led by the moderator using a guide of topic areas, and consists of an open discussion about the subject area. These discussions are audiotaped, sometimes transcribed, and used by the surveyor to develop questions for a survey. In this case, the focus groups were designed to test an existing questionnaire using cognitive questionnaire development techniques, which determine what respondents hear when asked a question and what they think the question is asking. The surveyor or moderator has the opportunity to determine how a question is processed in a one-on-one situation that closely resembles the interview process.

4 Format of the Questionnaire

Neophyte surveyors make two common errors in developing and formatting questionnaires: They indicate in instructions or cover letters that the questionnaire will "only take 5 minutes to fill out," and they format the questionnaire in ways to make it look shorter. Often, an unsophisticated surveyor will attempt to make the entire questionnaire fit on two sides of one page. The stated objective in both cases is "to increase response rates." Both are errors and, in fact, may *reduce* response rates for a number of reasons. If a research question is worth studying, data can rarely or never be collected from an individual in less than 5 minutes—regardless of how the data are collected. It takes 5 minutes to open the envelope and read the cover letter or introduction to the questionnaire!

If you have gone to all the trouble to develop a questionnaire, print it, and mail it, you want to make sure that you collect sufficient information to answer your research question. We know people who have eliminated demographic information from questionnaires because they wanted "to save space" only to discover during data analysis that their elimination of such information has made it impossible to answer certain important questions about their sample population.

Length

Surveyors squish all their questions onto two sides of one sheet of paper for the same reason. They want to make the questionnaire look shorter. But by doing this, they usually eliminate important information from their study, *or* they make the questionnaire unreadable. They leave no space between questions. Margins are small or nonexistent. The respondent needs a magnifying glass to see the print, and response categories are difficult to find or differentiate between.

In formatting a questionnaire, you want to "help" the respondent move through it. One of the most valuable things that can be done to help the respondent is to leave sufficient space between questions, between each question and the set of response categories, and between the alternative response categories. Space is as important as content in the presentation of a questionnaire. It has been suggested that mail questionnaires should be no longer than 12 pages; in general, most range between 4 and 12 pages. However, longer questionnaires can be used under two circumstances: when the respondents are highly motivated and when the reason for the additional number of pages is largely a function of increasing the questionnaire's readability.

Vertical Format

Notice in Figures 3–1 through 3–4 and 3–6 (Chapter 3) that we used a vertical format for our questions and answer categories. Other methods, such as shading, boxes, a newspaper column format, and arrows, exist for maximizing the clarity and order of a questionnaire. The 1990 Census, a page of which is reproduced in Figure 2–1 (Chapter 2), provides an example of a mail questionnaire where boxes and a newspaper column format are used to clarify how the respondent proceeds through the questionnaire.

We like a vertical format for two reasons. First, it simultaneously differentiates the question from the possible response categories and differentiates the response categories from each other. If, for example, we had used a horizontal format for Question 4 in Figure 3–2, we might have ended up with something like this:

In general, would you say your health is:
Excellent . . . 1 Very Good . . . 2 Good . . . 3 Fair . . . 4 or Poor . . . 5

or even this:

In general, would you say your health is:
____Excellent ____Very Good ____Good ____Fair or ____Poor

Many people think that respondents are unable to work with precoded questions such as those used in our examples. Instead, they have respondents put a check mark next to the appropriate answer category. Then, for reasons we have never been able to explain, they put the space for the check *in front of* the answer category *and*, to save space, use a horizontal format! What's wrong with this strategy?

First of all, we in the United States are used to filling out precoded questionnaires. We have no difficulty circling a number or filling in a box on a prescanned data form. Second, we read from left to right in English. Putting answer spaces or categories to the *left* of the word or phrase with which it corresponds is counterintuitive. Third, horizontal formatting of answer categories increases the errors made by respondents. In our preceding second example, a respondent can easily confuse the alternatives and put a check mark in the blank before "good" and that corresponds to an answer of "good" when what the respondent *really* intended to say was that his or her health was "very good." Similarly in the first example, even with the precoding and the dots linking the verbal response with the numeric code, the respondent may well select the number physically *closest* to the word rather than the code linked to it by dots.

Finally, a vertical format with codes already assigned and placed to the right of the response category makes data entry much easier and more error free. With most answers placed to the right of each page, the person doing data entry can simply go down the side of the page when entering the data.

The one exception to vertical format in our examples is shown in Questions 12 and 13 in Figure 3–1 (Chapter 3). Here, there are stem questions and then, instead of simply asking respondents to circle the numbers that correspond to the situations for which they use reading glasses, we ask them to select either "yes" or "no." We do it here because this is particularly important information in this study, and the inclusion of the yes/no column tends to increase the likelihood that the respondent will read each activity. A horizontal format similarly is used when a set of questions is all going to be answered using the same answer categories—for example, in a Likert-type format. Figure 4–1 provides an example.

1. The first set of questions asks about your overall vision **right now** during the past week. In answering these questions, answer in terms of your **usual** lens-wearing pattern during the past week.

In answering each question, use a range from one (1) to seven (7), where "1" stands for "strongly agree" and "7" stands for "strongly disagree." If you "strongly agree" with the statement, circle the "1"; if you agree less strongly, circle the "2," which stands for "agree pretty strongly," etc.

			Strongly Agree		Neutral				Strongly Disagree
V20	1)	I can see well far away **without** correction	1	2	3	4	5	6	7
V21	2)	When I drive at night, I have a lot of problems with glare from lights	1	2	3	4	5	6	7
V22	3)	If I drive in the morning I have to wear my lenses, but if I drive in the late afternoon (before dusk) I can drive without my lenses	1	2	3	4	5	6	7
V23	4)	I have a lot of trouble with glare in my operated eye(s)	1	2	3	4	5	6	7
V24	5)	When I read, I need more light than I used to	1	2	3	4	5	6	7
V25	6)	I hate wearing reading glasses	1	2	3	4	5	6	7
V26	7)	Without my lenses, I use one eye to look at things that are close to me and the other eye to look at things that are far away	1	2	3	4	5	6	7
V27	8)	Even with my usual lenses (if worn), my visual acuity is not as good at night as it is during the day	1	2	3	4	5	6	7

Figure 4–1. Example of a Likert-Type Scale With Variable Names

Grids

Both Figures 3–1 (Chapter 3) and 4–1 provide simple examples of what we call "grids." Grids enable a surveyor to save space on a questionnaire. They can be set up when a series of questions to be asked will use the same selection of answer categories. Grids are particularly popular for use in writing a series of questions to be used in developing a scale or index. They can also be used to format multiple sets of question sequences. Such grids are usually complicated and complex and, as such, difficult for a respondent to work through in a self-administered questionnaire. Thus, they are usually only used in interviewer-administered questionnaires.

Spacing

Notice that in our examples we have left substantial space between questions and response categories and used dots to clearly indicate which numeric code is associated with which answer. In these examples, we have used at least double-spacing between questions and between each question and its response categories. Within each set of answer categories we have used 1.5 spacing. Notice also that we have indented sets of answers under questions to help clarify where one question stops and the next begins. Where we have dependent questions—for example, 1A and 1B in Figure 3–2—these questions are similarly indented. This helps the respondent follow the skip instructions that correspond to the answer given to Question 1. Respondents who say "yes" are asked to answer Questions 1A and 1B, whereas those who say "no" are asked to go on to Question 2. The combination of indentation, spacing, and instructions that are set off—in this case, by capital letters—helps the respondent move expeditiously through the questionnaire.

Printing the questionnaire as a booklet, which consists of folding pages in the middle lengthwise and stapling them at the fold to form a "book," is a format we particularly like. When funds are available to do it, a questionnaire that is printed as a booklet looks more professional. We generally use 8½" × 17" paper for booklets because larger print can be used.

Often, the pages of a questionnaire are produced on a word processor and the size of the page then reduced during printing and production of the booklet. In the process, however, the print is also reduced. Small print or ornate print can be difficult for respondents to read, especially so for those over age 50 who need to wear reading glasses or who have difficulty seeing in poor light. We recommend using a 10-point pitch size and an easily read font with equal character spacing, such as Courier. Surveyors should avoid using italics, which are difficult to read, and fonts that use proportional spacing (i.e., the letter "m" takes up more space than "i"), as they can cause alignment problems (and can create extreme headaches) when setting up a questionnaire.

Print and Paper

There should be good contrast between the print and the paper. When in doubt, use black print on a white background. Some colors of paper, such as the currently fashionable neon colors, are difficult for respondents to look at for long periods of time. Also, colors that lower the contrast for color-blind persons should be avoided.

In our examples, we have used combinations of **bold,** <u>underlining,</u> and CAPITALS when we want to emphasize something in the text of a question or give an instruction about how to fill out the questionnaire. We consistently use capitals in providing instructions—for example, the instructions CIRCLE

ALL THAT APPLY, GO TO Q2, and ANSWER A. We use bold type and sometimes underlining to emphasize key words or phrases in a question—for example, **reading** and **close work** in Question 10 of Figure 3–1.

Other techniques, such as shading or boxing information, are also used. As we recommended earlier, italics should not be used because they are harder for a respondent to read, but other surveyors do use italics for emphasis or in instructions. We also find it problematic to put too much information in bold type. Some surveyors print all their instructions in bold. If a page contains a lot of instructions, the text of the question itself and the response categories tend to get lost, with the result that the respondent sees the instructions very well but tends to miss key phrases in the question or key answer alternatives.

Consistency

Whatever the size and format of print selected, the key is to be consistent. If the decision is that instructions contained within the body of the questionnaire are going to be underlined, then make sure you underline *all* the instructions in the body of the questionnaire and do *not* use underlining to provide emphasis in the text of a question. Rather, use bold type for emphasis.

Similar consistency should be used in the spacing between questions and in the use of indentations. If you decide to have single spacing in the text of a question and double spacing between questions, then be sure that you are consistent throughout the questionnaire. Notice that our examples are consistent in the way we line up the answer categories. In Figure 3–1 (Chapter 3), the text of all questions is indented, and the answer categories for all questions are similarly indented, with the beginning of each answer lined up and the respective codes lined up.

Splitting Questions Between Pages

A common error that new surveyors often make is to split a question between pages, to split the instructions for a section from the questions that it is describing, or to split related and dependent questions across pages. This often occurs in the interests of saving space or simply because the surveyor doesn't think. Take a moment to look at Figure 3–1 in Chapter 3. Imagine that there was sufficient space on a prior page for the instructions that precede Question 2 but insufficient space for the question itself. Some surveyors will go ahead and put the instructions on the prior page and then wonder why respondents subsequently have difficulty understanding the questions that follow on the next page.

Another common error is to place the instructions and Question 2 on one page because there is sufficient room but then to place Question 2A on a subsequent page. Because Question 2A is logically dependent on Question 2, this practice increases the probability that respondents never see Question 2A or that they do not understand it.

Finally, look at Question 12. Here, the two parts of the question are followed by long lists of possible responses. Yet another common error is to split this list of possible responses between two pages—again to save space. What happens is that respondents fail to see the complete list and, as a result, never read or consider those responses found on the second page. This is particularly problematic when respondents are asked to select a *single* response to the question. Because they do not equally weigh the possible answers on the second page with those seen on the first page, the result is a significantly lower number of persons selecting the responses on the second page.

Occasionally, a list is too long to be printed on a single page even if the question (e.g., Question 12) starts at the top of the page. In general, we recommend against using such long lists in a mail questionnaire. However, sometimes it is unavoidable. If lists must continue onto a second page, then the questionnaire *must* be printed in a booklet form, with the question itself and the first part of the list of responses on an even-numbered page and the continuation of the list on the facing odd-numbered page.

Checklist for Formatting Questionnaires

✓ **Do not make unrealistic time estimates.**

✓ **Ask enough questions to obtain the information needed.**

✓ **Use space between questions.**

✓ **Use vertical format, space, boxes, arrows, shading, or other devices consistently to maximize the clarity and order of questions.**

✓ **Do not avoid precoded response categories, but clearly indicate the code that corresponds to each response.**

✓ **Consider the use of simple grids.**

✓ **Use a booklet format when possible.**

✓ Have good contrast between print and paper.

✓ Use 10-point pitch.

✓ Use an easily read, equally spaced font, such as Courier.

✓ Avoid italics.

✓ Use bold, <u>underlining,</u> or CAPITALS judiciously and consistently for emphasis and instructions.

✓ Do not split instructions, questions, and associated responses between pages.

Coordinating With Data Entry Personnel and Data Processors

As questionnaires are being developed, the surveyor needs to consider the needs of persons who will be doing the data entry and data processing. We have already recommended that closed-ended questions be precoded with clear indications of where and how answers are to be recorded. We also recommend setting up the protocol by which the data will be entered into the computer prior to actually finalizing the questionnaire and then providing either variable names or column information on the questionnaire itself at the time it is printed.

Figure 4–1 provides an example of a set of questions where the data entry program was preset and the variable names that corresponded to each question in the data set were included on the questionnaire when it was printed. Some people object to having such information on questionnaires given to respondents on the grounds that this information is not understood by respondents and confuses them. In our own research, we have not noticed that such information reduces response rates or confuses respondents. Regardless of whether or not surveyors include such information on the form, they must, at minimum, ensure that the data being collected can be efficiently transferred into machine-readable form.

Ending the Questionnaire

The questionnaire should be ended by inviting respondents to comment on its content, to make suggestions about what might have been missed by the surveyor, and even to complain about the questionnaire itself. Such questions are often referred to as "ventilation" questions because they allow respondents to "ventilate" their feelings about the topic or the questionnaire.

Next, respondents should be given instructions for mailing back or returning the questionnaire. Stamped envelopes pre-addressed to the surveyor often get lost or mislaid. If an address is not provided on the questionnaire itself, respondents who have lost the envelope have no way of knowing how to return the questionnaire. Letting respondents return completed questionnaires by fax is an option that surveyors might consider.

Finally, respondents should be thanked for their time and cooperation. This is a courtesy due any study participant.

Camera-Ready Copy

If all of the above points have been considered and solved and the content carefully proofread for possible errors, the questionnaire is "camera ready," or ready for duplication and production. Usually, questionnaires are either photocopied or set up for offset printing. The details and costs of such procedures are discussed in Chapter 5.

Checklist for Finalizing the Questionnaire

✓ **Format to facilitate data entry.**

✓ **Afford respondents the opportunity to comment on the questionnaire.**

✓ **Make sure the return address is printed on a mail questionnaire.**

✓ **Thank respondents.**

✓ **Carefully proofread the questionnaire one final time.**

✓ **Duplicate or print the questionnaire.**

Correspondence and the Motivation of Respondents

All self-administered questionnaires must be accompanied by an explanation of the purposes and sponsorship of the study. When questionnaires are distributed to respondents at a single site or on a one-to-one basis, this explanation may partially be provided verbally, with the written explanation appearing on the first page of the questionnaire itself. Earlier, we provided such an example for the PERK Study. Because that questionnaire represented a 10-year follow-up to a study in which respondents had been contacted repeatedly, we did not repeat information about sponsorship in the introductory statement. However, most questionnaires represent the first contact with a respondent and are *not* distributed as part of a multiyear follow-up. Surveyors should always reconfirm, elaborate on, or repeat information in writing, even when some of the information is provided verbally.

Mail questionnaires must *always* be accompanied by a cover letter. Including a well-written cover letter with the questionnaire mailing that explains the purpose of the study, how and why the respondent was selected, and cites meaningful reasons for why a respondent should reply will help increase compliance. Stress how important it is for the individual to respond and how important that person is to your research. It is also beneficial to have the cover letter signed or endorsed by someone with positive name recognition for the respondents. For example, if your sample is composed of individuals belonging to a particular professional organization, having the president of the organization endorse the study may be helpful, unless it is thought that members of the organization distrust the leadership.

Fourteen kinds of information should be included or considered for inclusion in a cover letter or for use in motivating respondents:

1. Use of letterhead
2. Information about sponsorship
3. Dates
4. Salutation
5. Purpose of the study

6. Reasons why an individual's participation is important

7. Incentives to encourage respondent participation

8. Use of advance letters

9. How material incentives will be provided or distributed

10. Realistic estimate of the time required to complete the questionnaire

11. How and why the respondent was chosen

12. Explanation of confidentiality and how the data will be handled

13. Provision of a name and phone number to call for information

14. When and how to return the questionnaire

Figures 3–8 through 3–11 (Chapter 3) provide examples of an advance letter, an original cover letter, a modified cover letter, and a motivational flyer that were used in the Workplace Assault Study.

USE OF LETTERHEAD

The quality of presentation is important for stimulating respondent interest. Materials sent to respondents should be as attractive and professional looking as possible. Earlier, we described how different colors of paper, style of print, and format of the questionnaire affect response rate. In Chapter 5, we discuss the relative advantages of hand-addressing envelopes versus typing them and the use of stamps versus metered mail. Although most of these treatments seem to have little effect on response rates, the number of returns do increase slightly with special materials.

The use of letterhead is advocated by all surveyors because it helps establish the importance of the study, gives information about study sponsorship, and serves indirectly as a means of personalizing the contact with the respondent. The fact that the respondent is being contacted by a recognized, reputable organization serves to legitimate the importance of the study and the uniqueness of this particular respondent's position as a source of information. All of the examples in Figures 3–8 through 3–11 were printed on the letterhead of the respective locals of the Service Employees International Union (SEIU): The example advance letter was printed on Local 535 letterhead, and the example cover letters were printed on Local 660 letterhead. Use of SEIU letterhead identified the study as a union-sponsored activity and helped establish its legitimacy.

INFORMATION ABOUT SPONSORSHIP

All three letters (Figures 3–8 through 3–10 in Chapter 3) specifically stated who was conducting the study or sponsoring it. Because this was a joint activity of SEIU Locals 535 and 660 and the Southern California Injury Prevention Research Center (SCIPRC) located in the School of Public Health at the University of California, Los Angeles, *both* groups were noted as sponsors, and representatives of both groups signed both letters. Note that mailings to Local 535 members were signed by the president of the Social Services Chapter of SEIU Local 535, and that mailings to Local 660 members were signed by the general manager of Local 660. All letters were also signed by the senior author as a representative of the SCIPRC at UCLA's School of Public Health.

DATES

The importance of dates on cover letters and other mailings cannot be emphasized enough. Many surveyors simply neglect to put a date on letters or, alternatively, do not fully think out the sequence of administrative procedures (see Chapter 5). As a consequence, the date that appears on a cover letter, advance letter, or follow-up materials differs substantially from the actual date of mailing. It is important that the dates are either identical with or shortly precede the postmarked date on the envelope.

SALUTATION

If you have the capability, personalizing the inside address and salutation rather than using global salutations, such as "Dear Respondent," "Dear Resident," or "Dear _____ Member," increases respondents' sense of their importance as a respondent. This was not possible in the Workplace Assault Study because of insufficient resources. We were, however, able to personalize the outside envelope with the respondent's name and home address.

PURPOSE OF THE STUDY

Notice that all three letters (Figures 3–8 through 3–10) explain the purpose of the study. In the advance letter (Figure 3–8), the purpose is specified in Paragraph 2. In the final version of the cover letter, the purpose is specified in the first paragraph:

> . . . Little is really known about personal safety and security while at work. The Service Employees International Union, Local [660/535] is concerned about the risks its members may encounter on a day-to-day basis. In cooperation with . . . , we are conducting a study of workplace safety.

In the original cover letter (Figure 3-9), the purpose was similarly specified in the first paragraph, but remember that during the pretest we discovered problems that led us to soften and modify the stated purpose of the letter.

We also decided to shorten the introductory information in response to union officials' suggestions that we were providing too much information and that respondents were unlikely to read and comprehend so much verbiage. Both versions of the cover letter have been presented so that readers can see for themselves the kinds of changes we made.

REASONS WHY AN INDIVIDUAL'S PARTICIPATION IS IMPORTANT

In the final cover letter (Figure 3-10), the first and last sentence of the first paragraph describe why an individual's participation is important:

> **We need your help to improve personal safety on the job for Los Angeles County employees. . . . Results from this survey will help determine measures that could be taken to protect our members.**

These sentences reiterate information provided in the advance letter (Figure 3-8) where we explain that " . . . **your participation in the survey is very important . . .**" and that this information "**. . . has to come from you!**"

In the cover letter used for the pretest, an additional reason given for the importance of an individual's participation was the fact that it *was* a pretest. In the second paragraph, we stated that "based on your comments and suggestions, the questionnaire will be revised . . ." and, as we have already noted, revisions were indeed made after the pretest.

INCENTIVES TO ENCOURAGE
RESPONDENT PARTICIPATION

Incentives used to encourage respondent participation often overlap with information about the purpose of the study and how the respondent was selected for the study. That was the case in the Workplace Assault Study. In the final cover letter (Figure 3–10), we explained that

> . . . only a small proportion of Los Angeles County employees has been selected to participate, so your experiences and thoughts on the subject are very important. You will be representing many employees who are similar to yourself.

We also noted that the information will be used to improve workplace safety. Similar information was included in the advance letter (Figure 3–8):

> The results of this study will document the extent and nature of risks that our members encounter at work. Hopefully, future projects will address policies and practices intended to improve personal safety of . . . Los Angeles County workers.

Respondents can be motivated to respond in many ways. Response is always best when the subject matter of the study is on a topic that has some personal relevance for the respondents, or when respondents believe that by participating they are contributing to some other, greater good. These are the techniques used in the Workplace Assault Study.

Monetary or Material Incentives

Providing a monetary or material incentive to respond is another method of increasing response rates. Incentives such as money, pencils or pens, notepads, calendars, raffle tickets, and the like can be used to increase participation. Some surveyors prefer to enclose a gift with the first mailing as an incentive to complete and return the questionnaire; others use it as an inducement to respond, promising to send the gift once the completed questionnaire is received. If a raffle or lottery is used, the winner or winners are chosen from among those who responded.

There is some controversy over the use of incentives, such as money or a small gift, to increase response rates. Some surveyors believe that the data collected from individuals who receive incentives is unreliable. Their reasoning is that the use of incentives "buys" responses from individuals who normally would not respond and who will pay little or no attention to the import of the study when filling out the questionnaire, merely putting down any answer.

Other surveyors feel that the use of incentives is entirely credible and in some circumstances is the only way to obtain a satisfactory response rate. These surveyors argue that the incentive merely indicates to individuals that their time is valuable and worth compensation.

Whether or not to use an incentive is up to the individual surveyor. Another decision that must be made when giving incentives is whether to give them with all first attempts or to only give them to those individuals who participate. If you have decided to use an incentive other than cash, consideration should be given as to the universality of the appropriateness of the gift.

Other Forms of Motivation

We are sure that other surveyors have utilized an infinite variety of other methods in an effort to motivate respondents and increase response rates. In the Workplace Assault Study, we added a cover flyer to the mailing of the questionnaire (see Figure 3–11). This was developed as a result of the pilot test and at the suggestion of union officials. Our reasoning was that many potential respondents were not taking sufficient time to read the cover letter. As a result, motivations included in the cover letter were not being received by the potential respondent. The purpose of the flyer was to "catch" the respondent's attention. Notice that the flyer was printed in large and varied print, contained an appeal to what we perceived were respondents' concerns—namely, workplace safety—briefly emphasized the purpose of the study, and referenced the union.

The flyer was printed on canary yellow paper to catch the potential respondent's eye. As noted earlier, we do not recommend using colors like canary yellow for a questionnaire or a cover letter because it is too difficult for a respondent to read for any period of time, *but* such colors can be used productively for occasional emphasis and to catch a respondent's attention.

Offering to supply the respondent with an abbreviated copy of the survey results is sometimes used as a motivator. Respondents enjoy being able to compare their answers to the results and being part of a research project. This is a relatively inexpensive means of increasing response rates. However, this "reward" for responding should not be offered if there is any chance that you might not be able to provide it or if sending the results would occur so far in the future that respondents won't remember the study.

USE OF ADVANCE LETTERS

Occasionally, the surveyor finds it profitable to send a letter or place a telephone call to the selected respondent in advance of the questionnaire being mailed. Although this usually is not possible in group self-administered situations, there are instances where the individuals can be informed that they will be part of a study at some future date. For example, employers can notify workers or teachers can tell students that they will be part of a study at a particular time and place and give them an idea of the study purpose. If you are using a letter or telephone call, it should introduce the study and give some brief information about it while alerting the respondent that he or she has been chosen as one of the special individuals who will receive the mailing within a few days.

An advance letter (Figure 3–8) was used in the Workplace Assault Study. The decision to have an advance letter was made as a result of the pilot study.

HOW MATERIAL INCENTIVES
WILL BE PROVIDED OR DISTRIBUTED

In the Workplace Assault Study, the question of whether or not to use monetary or material incentives was moot; we simply did not have sufficient resources to consider this option. If such incentives are to be used, the process by which and the circumstances under which the respondent will receive the incentive must be described in either the cover letter or an advance letter or both. In another study conducted by a UCLA professor, an award of $50 was provided by lottery to four students who returned a questionnaire that examined the social attitudes of American college students and compared them with those of peers in other countries. The cover letter was headed **WIN $50!!**, and the procedure was described in the body of the letter as follows:

As an added incentive, we will award $50 each to four students returning a completed questionnaire. The winning students will be chosen at random from the pool of those returning a fully completed questionnaire to us. In order to award the $50 prizes, we need to know which students returned the questionnaire and which students did not. To ensure confidentiality, this information will not be associated with the students' questionnaires. To accomplish this, you will place your completed questionnaire inside of the plain, unmarked envelope and mail this envelope to us. You will notice that the larger envelope has a number in the lower left-hand corner. This will tell us that you have returned a questionnaire. At this point your outer envelope will be destroyed and the inner envelope containing your completed questionnaire will be placed in a separate pile. Thus, it will not be possible to associate a given name with a given questionnaire. Your confidentiality will then be assured.

Notice that these instructions provide information on how confidentiality will be ensured while still allowing for provision of a cash incentive.

REALISTIC ESTIMATE OF THE TIME REQUIRED TO COMPLETE THE QUESTIONNAIRE

The surveyor should provide either a direct or an indirect estimate of the time required to complete the questionnaire. When the surveyor has determined just how long the questionnaire will take the *average respondent* to complete and the questionnaire is relatively short, then a direct estimate of the time needed can be provided. We stress "average respondent" because people differ in the amount of time they take and also differ as to whether they complete the questionnaire at one sitting or over multiple sittings. If an exact time estimate is given, the surveyor should clearly indicate that this represents only an average: Some respondents will take less time and some will take more time. An estimate of time needed should only be given after thorough pretesting and pilot work have been completed.

When surveyors anticipate that a questionnaire will take longer or may necessitate more thought on the part of respondents, it is better to indirectly indicate the probable time needed. This is what we chose to do in both the Workplace Assault Study and the PERK Study. In the cover letter for the assault study (Figure 3–10), we itemized the kinds of information we sought to collect—namely, the type of work they do and the place where they work, personal safety measures at their worksite, how safe or unsafe they feel at work, and their experience with workplace threats and assaults. We then went on to ask respondents to "please take the time to complete the questionnaire and return it in the enclosed self-addressed stamped envelope."

In the PERK Study (Figure 3–5), we similarly itemized the kinds of information to be collected and, in the third paragraph, assured respondents that "we have arranged for you to have enough time to finish the questionnaire before we start your vision testing."

The reason for using indirect methods to indicate the length of time needed in both of these studies was because we knew, for example, that in the Workplace Assault Study, those who had experienced assaults or threats would take significantly longer to complete the questionnaire but that the "average" respondent would not have had such experiences and would therefore not need a lengthy period of time. Thus, the range of time needed across the sample was broad but skewed toward less time.

In contrast, in the PERK Study, we knew from prior experience that respondents took about 25-30 minutes to complete the questionnaire; the respondents also knew that. Because we were careful to provide adequate time and resources for completing the questionnaire, we saw no reason to state a time in the introduction.

HOW AND WHY THE RESPONDENT WAS CHOSEN

Respondents are chosen in many different ways. In the Workplace Assault Study, respondents were selected randomly after union lists were prestratified according to job classification. Ten strata were created, and either 175 or 188 union members were selected from each stratum regardless of the number of persons in it. For purposes of the cover letter, it was not necessary to attempt to explain stratification to the respondents or exactly how randomization was achieved. It *was* important to emphasize that only some union members were being asked to complete the questionnaire, that these persons had been selected randomly, and that their responses were important because they represented others like themselves. This information appears in the first two sentences of the advance letter (Figure 3–8) and is described in more detail in the second paragraph of the cover letter (Figure 3–10) as follows:

> You have been randomly selected from the membership list of Local 660's Los Angeles County employees to participate in this survey. Only a small proportion of Los Angeles County employees has been selected to participate, so your experiences and thoughts on the subject are very important. **You will be representing many employees who are similar to yourself.**

In other studies, such as the PERK Study, everyone in a population receives the questionnaire. This is briefly referenced in the second paragraph of Figure 3–5 (Chapter 3) as follows:

> . . . In order to get accurate information about radial keratotomy and how it affects people's vision, we need information from **all** PERK patients. So please help us by answering the questions to the best of your ability.

EXPLANATION OF CONFIDENTIALITY
AND HOW THE DATA WILL BE HANDLED

Both federal law and research ethics require that subjects of all research studies be provided with information about how the collected data will be used and how their privacy or the confidentiality of their data will be ensured. In self-administered questionnaires, advance letters, cover letters, and introductory instructions provide the best occasion for describing this information. In some studies, the collected data are truly anonymous in that no effort is made to log responses or contact nonrespondents. That was not the case in either of the two example studies.

As part of a long-term, ongoing study where questionnaires were filled out at a clinical site, PERK respondents clearly were identifiable. Furthermore, during analyses, questionnaire data were linked to ophthalmic measures of vision. At the same time, it was important that we provide as much confidentiality and anonymity to respondents as was possible within the requirements of the study. This was in our interests and in the interests of the respondents to maximize the probabilities that respondents' answers were honest and complete. As we noted earlier, one of the major issues was to assure respondents that the information collected would not be available to personnel at the clinical site and would not affect their health care. The last sentence in Figure 3–5 (Chapter 3) describes what respondents should do to ensure confidentiality: "When you are **finished** with the questionnaire, **seal** the questionnaire in the attached envelope." . . .

In the Workplace Assault Study, we had had no prior contact with the respondents, so we emphasized the confidentiality of the data and clearly specified that no information would be released to respondents' employers (see Figure 3–10). Furthermore, we increased confidence in our assurances of confidentiality by sending questionnaires to respondents' home addresses (not work) and by having questionnaires returned to UCLA rather than to the union offices. We were unable to guarantee anonymity from the research staff because we did indeed plan to follow up on nonrespondents. We also included questions at the end of the questionnaire that asked persons to volunteer for follow-up interviews and included code numbers on the outside of each return envelope.

PROVISION OF A NAME AND PHONE NUMBER TO CALL FOR INFORMATION

Respondents always must be provided with a name and phone number of someone who will be available to answer questions about the questionnaire. This person should be accessible, be able to answer questions, send additional copies of the questionnaire, or respond to other requests the respondents may have. Often, this will be the person or persons who sign the cover letter. In the case of the Workplace Assault Study, we provided the name of Deborah Riopelle, the project manager who was located at UCLA, and that of a recognized member of the union staff.

There are always potential respondents who will call to verify the purpose or sponsorship of a study to assure themselves that the organization is legitimate or that confidentiality will be maintained. Other potential respondents will have questions about the content of the questionnaire or how their name was selected for the sample. If no name and number are listed to call, the respondent is unlikely to complete and return the questionnaire. Whenever possible, we recommend offering the respondent the option of calling the project collect. Unfortunately, this was not possible in the Workplace Assault Study because telephones within the University of California cannot be set up to accept collect calls, and we were unable to provide a non-University number for respondents to contact.

WHEN AND HOW TO RETURN THE QUESTIONNAIRE

Many surveyors include in the cover letter a deadline for returning the completed questionnaire. This can work either way: The respondent may be motivated to complete the form and return it immediately so as not to miss the deadline, or, if the packet is put aside and picked up close to the deadline or after the deadline, respondents may believe that it is too late to respond. In the Workplace Assault Study, we attempted to go between the horns of this dilemma by giving a deadline date but providing latitude in the way we stated it. For example, "It would be very helpful to have your completed questionnaire returned to us by January 25, 1995."

The cover letter asked respondents to return the questionnaire "in the enclosed self-addressed stamped envelope." Remember that earlier we also strongly recommended that the return address be placed at the end of the questionnaire itself in case the questionnaire gets separated from the envelope.

Checklist for Motivating
Respondents and Writing Cover Letters

✓ **Explain the purpose of the study.**

✓ **Describe who is sponsoring the study.**

✓ **Consider sending an advance letter.**

✓ **Consider using other methods such as newsletters or flyers to publicize the study.**

✓ **Include a cover letter with the questionnaire.**

- Use letterhead.
- Date the letter to be consistent with the actual date of mailing or administration.
- Provide a name and phone number for the respondent to contact for further information.
- Personalize the salutation, if feasible.
- Maximize the attractiveness and readability of the letter.

✓ **Explain how respondents were chosen and why their participation is important.**

✓ **Explain when and how to return the questionnaire.**

✓ **Describe incentives, if used.**

✓ **Directly or indirectly provide a realistic estimate of the time required by the average respondent to complete the questionnaire.**

✓ **Explain how the confidentiality of the respondents' data will be protected.**

✓ **Determine whether and how a deadline date will be provided for returning questionnaires.**

Writing Questionnaire Specifications

Once a questionnaire has been finalized, the surveyor should write questionnaire specifications. Questionnaire specifications provide the first major documentation about the study, what its objectives were, who the respondents were, how the questionnaire was administered, how follow-up was conducted, how completed questionnaires were processed, and the reason that each question or set of questions was included in the questionnaire. Surveyors frequently feel that once they have completed the design and administration of a study they cannot possibly forget any detail of its creation or the decisions made.

In fact, substantial amounts of time can pass before collected data are actually analyzed or written up. Sometimes, surveyors run out of money to complete the study in a timely fashion. Sometimes, other competing activities or research projects necessitate the postponement of the study's completion. Sometimes, the original people involved with the study leave the organization to take other jobs. We personally know of situations where it has taken as long as 10 years for a study to be completed! Even when such interruptions do not occur, it behooves the conscientious surveyor to document the decisions made in constructing and administering the questionnaire.

At minimum, questionnaire specifications should include information about the objective of the study, the selection and tracking of the sample, the number and timing of administrations and follow-up procedures, and the sources and reasons for each question.

When questionnaires are administered by interview, specifications are reduced to "interviewer specifications," which are used in training interviewers and for interviewers to use as reference in the field.

OBJECTIVE OF THE STUDY

The specifications should briefly summarize the purpose of the study. In the specifications for the PERK Study, the objective of its questionnaire was stated as follows:

> **Objective:** The 10-year questionnaire has three objectives. First, it allows us to get systematic information from patients at all the nine sites about problems they might have had, their current vision, and the current lens-wearing patterns. Second, it allows us to compare patients with themselves at baseline and at 1, 2, and 6 years after radial keratotomy on their first eye. Third, it allows us to compare the health of PERK patients to other, more representative samples of the United States' population.

Notice that the questionnaire had three objectives. The first objective was one that necessitated the collection of "new" or original data from this questionnaire, but the second and third objectives imply that some of the questions on the questionnaire will be adopted or adapted from past PERK questionnaires or other sources that will enable the data collected to be compared with existent data sets. The specification of these three objectives already alerts the reader as to the kind of questions that will be asked and the fact that some of the questions on this questionnaire are not original but are drawn from other studies.

SELECTION AND TRACKING OF THE SAMPLE

In the PERK Study, the questionnaire was given to *all* participants in the clinical trial as soon as they entered the clinical center for their 10-year examination. No effort was made to administer to patients who did not come in for this follow-up examination.

In contrast, in the Workplace Assault Study, union personnel randomly selected between 175 and 188 members from each of 10 job categories in the two locals.[1] This resulted in 1,763 names. Insufficient addresses existed for 19 of these names so they were immediately eliminated from the sample.

On January 5 and 6, 1995, advance letters were sent to the remaining 1,744 persons. On January 17, 1995, packets containing the questionnaire, a cover letter, a flyer, and an envelope for returning the questionnaire were mailed to the same 1,744 persons, which we considered our sample. On January 24, 1995, reminder postcards were sent to these persons, regardless of whether or not they had returned the questionnaire (see Figure 3–7 in Chapter 3). Then, on March 4 through 6, 1995, a second questionnaire with a new cover letter was sent to the 1,143 persons who had failed to respond to our first two mailings but for whom addresses appeared to be correct. Note that the new cover letter repeated some of the same information given before but added a section that emphasized the importance of getting responses from people who were *not* assaulted or who did *not* perceive their workplaces to be unsafe (see Figure 4–2). Finally, in April 1995, we began contacting by telephone those who still had not responded.

SOCIAL SERVICES
UNION

AMERICAN
FEDERATION
OF NURSES

309 SO. RAYMOND
AVENUE
PASADENA
CALIFORNIA
91105
818-796-0051
FAX 818-796-2335

February 21, 1995

Dear Member,

About four weeks ago we sent you a questionnaire about personal safety and security while at work. As of today, we have not yet received your completed questionnaire.

The Service Employees International Union, Local 535 is conducting this study of workplace safety in cooperation with the Southern California Injury Prevention Research Center at UCLA because of concerns members have expressed about personal safety while at work. Results from this survey will help determine measures that could be taken to protect Local 535 members.

You may feel that because your safety at work has not been threatened you don't need to reply. This is not true. By hearing about the experiences of all Local 535 members we can develop a better idea of which situations are safer than others. We are writing to you again because of the importance **each** questionnaire has to the study. **We need your completed questionnaire.**

We recognize how busy you must be and greatly appreciate you taking the time to complete this questionnaire. If by chance you did not receive the first questionnaire or it got misplaced, we have enclosed a replacement. It would be very helpful to have your completed questionnaire returned to us by **March 3, 1995**.

<u>Your responses are confidential.</u> **No names or individual information will be used or released to your employer.** If you have any questions or concerns, please feel free to call Deborah Riopelle, M.S.P.H. at UCLA, (310) 555-4053 or Wilma Cadorna at Local 535 at 818-555-0051.

Sincerely,

Jerry L. Clyde   Linda Bourque, Ph.D.
President, Social Services Chapter   UCLA School of Public Health
SEIU Local 535

Figure 4–2.   Example of Cover Letter Directed to Respondents as Part of Second Full Mailing (Nonresponders)

All of the above information, starting with how the sample was selected and why it was selected that way and ending with response rates by time of contact and job category, is documented in the questionnaire specifications. Thus, when we get ready to analyze and write up our findings, we can quickly go to the Questionnaire Specifications to refresh our memory about how and why we selected the sample we did, the kind of response we obtained at each stage of the mailing, and the extent to which response rates differed by job stratum.

TIMING OF ADMINISTRATION

The above section also documents the *timing* of contacts with the sample. In the PERK Study, the questionnaire was given out only once, and every effort was made to ensure that clinic personnel obtained a completed questionnaire from each respondent.

In contrast, in the Workplace Assault Study, respondents were contacted a minimum of three times (advance letter, first mailing of questionnaire, and follow-up postcard) and a maximum of five or more times (advance letter, first mailing of questionnaire, follow-up postcard, second mailing of questionnaire, and one or more phone calls).

By keeping track of *when* a respondent responded relative to the timing and number of the contact, the surveyor can assess various things about the sample—for example, whether responsiveness varies with job category, gender, age, perceptions of vulnerability in the workplace, or actual experiences of physical assault.

INSTRUCTIONS FOR ADMINISTERING QUESTIONS

Once the timing and method of contacting respondents had been specified for the Workplace Assault Study, no further administrative requirements had to be outlined in the specifications.

In contrast, in the PERK Study, the specifications contained instructions to the clinical coordinator for administering the questionnaire as follows:

ADMINISTRATION
OF THE QUESTIONNAIRE

TIME:

Allow at least 30 minutes for the patient to fill out the questionnaire. If you interview any patients over the phone, make sure that they have the time to do it. You may want to call them and arrange a special time for you to conduct the interview.

SITE:

Provide each patient with a quiet room or secluded area in the general waiting room. Provide them with a pencil or pen, table or clipboard, and the envelope in which to put the completed questionnaire.

OTHER PEOPLE:

Discourage other people from "helping" the patient fill out the questionnaire. If you interview them, try to do it at a time when they will not be interrupted by family or colleagues and at a time when they have no other things to do.

EMPHASIZE:

We want to know about **their experiences** with radial keratotomy and how they feel about things. There are no "right" or "wrong" answers, and patients should not try to please you with the answer they give. We **expect** to find variations in opinions and experiences.

In general, remember that **we need their opinions** of their vision, not our observations about what we think their vision is. Please give them enough time to think about their answers and avoid hurrying them through the questionnaire. If patients do not like our alternatives, encourage them to write down their feelings or experiences and we will evaluate the information they provide.

COVER PAGE:	The cover page provides the patient with a brief description of the information that the questionnaire is designed to collect. As you give the questionnaire to the patient, direct his or her attention to the second and third paragraphs in particular. These describe how the data will be used and tell the patient what to do when he or she has completed the questionnaire.
COORDINATOR:	Before giving the questionnaire to the patient, please make sure that the patient's identification number is on every page of the questionnaire and that the date of administration is filled out on the cover page.

Notice that the above instructions are formatted in a way to make it easier for the survey administrator to find information on a particular subject, and that every effort is made to encourage the clinic coordinator *not* to interfere with the patient while he or she is filling out the questionnaire. This is particularly important when the persons administering a questionnaire are not professional interviewers. In the same way that surveyors must try to recognize and compensate for their own biases, they also need to try to anticipate the biases of others who may be involved in the collection of data.

QUESTIONS RAISED BY RESPONDENTS

In the same way that questionnaire specifications attempt to anticipate the attitudes and behaviors of data collectors, surveyors need to try to anticipate questions or challenges that respondents may direct to a data collector. Whenever possible, data collectors should be given information that helps them answer such questions or handle such challenges. The following information was included in the specifications for the PERK Study:

QUESTIONS RAISED
BY THE PATIENT

Questions asked about the questionnaire will probably be of two types: a question of clarification or a question designed to have **you** provide the information or **your** opinion about their vision.

CLARIFICATION:	If a patient does not understand a question, try to find out what it is that he or she does not understand and try to find a synonym or another way to say it. Please make a note of the question asked and let Portia Griffin at Emory know about it.
NO APPROPRIATE ANSWER AVAILABLE:	If a patient cannot represent him/herself with the answers available, tell him or her to write down an answer that **does** represent his or her feelings or experiences.
CHALLENGES:	If a subject starts to challenge the objective of the questionnaire or a particular item in it, or says that it is repetitive, etc., please listen, be polite, and be noncommittal. **Do not give** patients the answers or indicate that you will let them stop answering the questions.

Source and Reason for Questions

The major historical purpose of questionnaire specifications has been to document the source and reason for including a question or set of questions in an instrument. Figure 4–3 provides an example of the specifications from the PERK Study, which describes Questions 2 through 12 (see Figure 3–1, Chapter 3), Questions 43 through 45, and Questions 54 through 61 (see Figure 3–3).

Notice that specifications may be provided for sets of questions (e.g., Q2-25), subsets of questions (Q2-7, Q9-13, Q43-45, and Q54-65), or for individual questions (e.g., Q9, Q10, Q11, and Q12). Each specification describes what the purpose of the question or questions is and whether it replicates or revises an earlier question or, by implication, indicates that it is a new question. For example, Questions 2 through 7 replicate questions that were asked in earlier PERK questionnaires and the RAND Health Insurance Experiment. In contrast, Questions 9 through 13 are new to this questionnaire because this is the first time that we are assessing presbyopia, or a person's increased inability to see things that are close as he or she ages.

Questions 43 through 45 also replicate questions that were used in other PERK questionnaires and in the HIE. In the case of these questions, however, data collected were reported in an earlier article. The fact that this occurred is documented as part of the specification, and complete citations are provided for those articles. This reminds the surveyor at a later time that these earlier analyses had occurred and provides a quick reference as to where to find information about them.

In general, if a specification cannot be written for *why* a question exists, then there probably is no reason to have the question on the questionnaire.

PERK 10-Year Questionnaire
August 17, 1992

LENS-WEARING PATTERNS:

Q2-25   Questions 2-25 ask patients to tell us about their current lens-wearing patterns.

Q2-7   Questions 2-7 were used in both the baseline and 6-year questionnaires to measure patients' functional vision. These questions are similar to questions used in RAND's Health Insurance Experiment and a wide range of other studies where vision has been assessed. We are repeating them so that we can see what kind of effect radial keratotomy has had on their functional vision. The questions on presbyopia and distant vision that were added to Question 1 above represent an effort to improve the precision of information traditionally collected exclusively with Questions 6 and 7.

Q8   In evaluating how presbyopia affects the eyes of persons who have had radial keratotomy, we realized that we have no way of identifying patients who might have been presbyopic at baseline. Question 8 provides an opportunity to get a rough estimate of this.

Q9-13   Questions 9-13 assess whether patients have become or are becoming presbyopic and how presbyopia is affecting both their vision and their use of lenses. These questions can also be used in assessing how severe overcorrection affects the daily vision of PERK patients.

Q9   Ascertains whether the patient was told about presbyopia in the context of the PERK Study.

Q10   Ascertains whether the patient is presbyopic and whether presbyopia has necessitated the use of spectacles for near vision.

Q11   Ascertains when presbyopia resulted in the use of spectacles.

Q12   A number of situations are listed in Question 12. Patients are asked to respond for **each eye.** By looking at the pattern of responses to Question 12, we will be able to assess to what degree patients are disabled by presbyopia or severe overcorrection of their vision.

.
.
.
.

(continued)

Q43-45   These three questions were in both the baseline and 6-year questionnaires. Originally included in RAND's Health Insurance Experiment, data obtained with these questions were reported in Borque, Rubenstein, Cosand et al., Psychological characteristics of candidates for the Prospective Evaluation of Radial Keratotomy, <u>Archives of Ophthalmology</u> 1984; 102:1187-1192. Inclusion of these questions will allow us to compare the patients both to themselves at earlier points in time and to RAND myopes.

.
.
.
.
.

Q54-65   Questions 54-65 provide us with information about how and when PERK patients use their eyes to read, drive, watch television, and participate in sports and other physical activities. The number and type of activities done as well as the time of day at which they are done may influence their need for and use of lenses.

Figure 4–3.   Example of Questionnaire Specification

Checklist for Writing
Questionnaire Specifications

✓ **Briefly describe the objective of the study.**

✓ **Describe the study sample and response rates.**

✓ **Describe any tracking done of the sample.**

✓ **Describe timing of data collection and tracking.**

✓ **Provide instructions for administering questionnaires.**

✓ **Provide answers for data collectors to use in response to anticipated questions.**

✓ **Index specifications for easy reference.**

✓ **Describe why a question is asked.**

✓ **If questions are adopted or adapted from other studies, explain the reasons for such decisions and provide complete citations to the other studies.**

Note

1. Nine strata were selected from Local 660, the largest local, and 175 names were randomly selected within each stratum. The population of each group at the time of the sample draw was as follows: Public Social Services, 6,208; Public Health Department, 1,336; Public Library, 309; Probation, 578; Sheriff's Department, 908; Parks and Recreation, Animal Care and Control, and Public Works, 922; Assessor's Office, Children's Services, and Treasurer and Tax Collector Offices, 1,625; Municipal and Superior Courts, 1,067; and Hospitals, 3,501. Only 3,221 members of Local 535 work in Los Angeles County, with the largest group being the 2,090 in the Department of Social Services; 188 persons were randomly selected from this stratum.

5 Implementation

The implementation of self-administered and mailed surveys requires considerable coordination and attention to detail. This multistage process begins with sample selection and ends with the processing of the last of the returned and completed questionnaires.

In this chapter, we discuss issues associated with the identification and selection of the sample as well as the material costs and staffing needs associated with self-administered and mailed surveys. We elaborate on the processes involved in coordinating self-administered surveys, or in the case of mailed surveys, preparing packets for mailing, posting these packets, subsequent follow-up and return of packets, and procedures typically used for the tracking of envelopes returned

135

due to unknown addressee or no such address. Actual examples of expected expenditures and person hours are provided.

Developing and Producing the Sample

Typically, a self-administered or mailed survey is considered only when the investigator is confident that the desired sample population is accessible at a designated location. This survey methodology is often the only efficient means of obtaining data from a somewhat rare population. When the goal of a survey is to collect data about individuals with a characteristic that is not common in the population, this is known as a rare population. For example, say a major motorcycle manufacturer wanted to test the acceptance of a new concept in handle bars by the motorcycle-riding public. The easiest approach might be to mail a survey to members of motorcycle clubs or to hand out questionnaires at large motorcycle distributorships or motorcycle repair shops.

These characteristics of groups sampled for self-administered questionnaires can be further refined by even greater selectivity of the location of administration. For example, if the purpose of the study is to determine the types of baby products used by mothers of infants, a quick and easy sample source would be to conduct self-administered surveys with parents in the waiting rooms of well-baby clinics. In short, samples can be gathered from many sources such as waiting rooms, a line in a place of business, a classroom, a home address, a place of employment, or a temporary residence, such as a school dormitory or a hospital room. Self-administered surveys conducted in this manner are known as convenience samples and are generally used as a means of getting data easily and quickly from highly specialized populations. In many instances, a self-administered survey eliminates what would otherwise be an overwhelming effort and cost to locate at random particular types of individuals within the general population.

Mail surveys are often sent to members of professional, political, religious, or social organizations; employees within a particular institution or job classification; students; subscribers to newsletters and magazines; and consumers of particular products or services. Again, a major consideration in favor of using a mailed survey is the appreciably lower cost of locating appropriate populations.

Not all self-administered or mailed surveys are conducted because of the ease of finding a rare population, however. Frequently, this method is chosen because it is far less expensive to conduct than is a telephone or face-to-face survey. Additionally, mailed surveys can sometimes be more successful at getting data from hard-to-reach populations such as doctors, business executives, and politicians.

There are certain caveats to consider when evaluating a mailed survey coming from certain sources. For example, if you are considering using addresses and/or names and addresses obtained from telephone directories, you should first consider the approximate mobility of the population under consideration and the rate of unlisted households in the area. If you are mailing to specific names in the telephone book, you should determine the rate of turnover in telephone number ownership, that is, how many people are likely to change their telephone number by the time you use the directory for a sample. Obviously, this will result in undelivered or unanswered mail.

It is also wise to determine from your local telephone company the proportion of households with unlisted numbers. If the number is not listed, that household will have no opportunity to be included in the survey and will therefore be underrepresented in the population. If having an unlisted telephone number is typical of particular population types, such as the elderly, those with a high income, or single females, your sample will be biased away from that portion of the population. In some cities, such as Los Angeles, the unlisted rate is around 60% of the households, whereas in less urban areas, it can drop below 20%. A different twist on this problem is households with the telephone number listed in the directory but with the street address suppressed. Regardless of the source, you should always try to determine how your sample might be biased due to lack of inclusion.

SAMPLE AVAILABILITY

When a self-administered survey is to be conducted in a group setting, permission to access this population must be obtained from the institution where these individuals are. In the case of the well-baby clinic, we would need permission from the hospital or medical director of the establishment to approach the patients. Likewise with the motorcycle club members, we would need to be granted access to these individuals by the executive level of the club or clubs. For dealerships or repair shops, we would also need owner permission to approach customers on the premises.

In some instances, it may be necessary for the organization granting the access to obtain informed consent from the individuals to be studied, prior to allowing you access. In most cases, with mailed surveys, the name and address of the sampled individual is recorded and available in some electronic medium. Obviously, access to these files is not possible without proper authorization. Permission to access the data banks or lists must be obtained from the organization.

The fees for samples can vary considerably. When working with groups or organizations who are either sponsoring the research or are interested in the results, you may simply be asked to cover the cost of materials (i.e., labels and machine time), or you may have to pay for both the labor and materials required to program and process your request.

In some instances, the cooperating organization may provide the labels free of charge and, not uncommonly, will help defray part or all of the mailing costs. Typically, the association should be able to provide either addressed mailing labels or raw data on some compatible computer medium. There are publishing companies who specialize in the compilation and production of directories of government officials and employees, corporate officials, business firms within professions, and the like.

In other instances, the focal point of the research may be on types of individuals with particular sociodemographic or socioeconomic characteristics. The addressee may be known, or the survey may have to be sent to an anonymous "resident" or "occupant." In a situation such as this, a sample may be purchased from a directory publisher, commercial bulk-mailing establishment, or specialized marketing firm. These organizations have compiled mailing addresses within certain demographic domains. Often, U.S. Census data are linked to ZIP codes so that samples can be focused on neighborhoods where households with particular characteristics are more likely to exist, such as married senior citizens with annual incomes over $30,000. Many organizations involved in providing address samples supplement the data with information they have gathered from other sources, such as sales profiles from department or grocery stores, newspaper readership, and other surveys conducted in the area.

In today's computer-based environment, the amount of information available about each of us is at times very disconcerting. When using purchased samples, keep in mind that they are not necessarily representative of the general population and may be subject to innumerable biases.

List samples can often be unreliable. They may be out-of-date—that is, they do not have current address and/or telephone number information on an individual—or they may not contain all the candidates possible for inclusion in the study. Lists can be up-to-date and inclusive and still contain clerical errors that will cause problems reaching the respondent. It is always a good idea to spot-check your sample before using it—for example, mailing to a few addresses, making some telephone calls, or comparing list information to another source, such as the telephone directory.

SELECTING THE SAMPLE

When administrating a questionnaire at a site such as a grocery store, you may want to ask all individuals encountered to fill out the form, or you may want to select a subsample of these individuals. If you decide on a subsample, you need to determine a means of representatively selecting respondents rather than taking only the first group to appear. Ideally, you want to spread your sample out evenly over times of day, days of the week, or types of individuals. A commonly used means of selecting respondents is to determine a sampling interval.

For example, assume that 1,000 parents of infants come into the well-baby clinics in our sample in any given week. We have decided that we want to interview only 200 of them. To spread the sample across the entire week's population, we would approach every fifth client who comes for well-baby care. This is known as a sampling interval. This method of selection provides a systematically selected sample within a given time period and place.

If a subgroup within the general sample population is of interest, such as people between 35 and 55 years of age or African Americans, you will want to select the respondents at different sampling intervals to ensure that you obtain data from a sufficient number of individuals for each group you want to compare. This is called stratified systematic sampling.

In some group settings, such as clinics or classrooms, you may be able to preselect respondents from patient charts or class rosters. Again, you will need permission to gain access to these records. If a list is not available, you will have to determine another means of selecting respondents, such as the order in which they signed in or entered the room.

Selecting a mailing sample uses essentially the same process. If not using the whole list (or universe), you will want to give instructions to the processor as to how to select the sample using a sampling interval. When selecting or drawing samples it is a common practice to start at a random starting point in the list and, using a constant interval, rotate from the bottom around to the top of the list and down to the initial starting point. If, for example, we have a list of 1,000 mothers who bring their babies to a clinic and we want to send questionnaires to 200, we select a random start point—say, woman #322 on the list—and then take every fifth woman on the list (e.g., 327, 332, 337, etc.). Again, if the data file contains individual data on characteristics of particular interest, you want to draw the sample with different sampling intervals for different types of individuals.

ADDRESSING THE MAILING

There are three methods for putting the sample address on the mailing packet. Addresses can be handwritten on the envelopes, typed or printed directly on them, or labels affixed to them. There has been some research indicating a nonsignificant increase in the rate of returns with hand-addressed envelopes. Similarly, machine-printed envelopes are received a bit more favorably than those with labels affixed. Unless the sample size is extremely small, say, a few hundred, the intensive labor involved in hand-addressing envelopes does not warrant this approach. Similarly, if the sample file must be created by hand-typing, it would be wiser to spend this clerical time entering the information into a computer file so that it is available for subsequent mailings.

As a final precaution, with much of the mail being optically scanned today, it is wise to check with your local post office to determine if there are any specific layout restrictions on bulk mailing. As an example, we discovered that if more than four spaces occurred between the last number of the street address and the street name, the post office scanner stopped reading at the unit number and found the address "incomplete." When you lay out your data field for addressing, be sure that the address length and width conforms to the size of your mailing labels.

PLANNING THE SAMPLE FILE

When providing specifications for the sample format or label layout, consider how many mailings you plan to send to each respondent. If the sample file is not easily accessible, you will want to have all the necessary materials run at the same time. For example, if you plan an initial mailing and two follow-ups, ask for three copies of the labels to be run along with a hard-copy printout of the sample. This will eliminate the need to return to the supplier and ask for additional label runs and will give you a master copy of the sample against which you can log in your returns.

This can save costs in the long run because typically a substantial part of the cost in running address labels is in the initial set-up time or programming. Thus, requesting additional sets of labels on the initial run adds only to the cost of materials and not to the cost of labor. If for some reason you cannot obtain more than one set of address labels, most copying machines can generate label sheets if the original label format is a standard three addresses across.

If you are running the address labels from within your own organization and there is no problem with access, you probably will not want to run all the sets at one time. If you are going to have the postal service send back address corrections, or you plan to do tracking on bad addresses, you will want to make these changes or corrections to your master file before you produce the next batch of labels. Additionally, if you are logging in the completed returns, you will have eliminated labels for these respondents and for those who are lost to follow-up (deceased, no useable address, etc.).

Another consideration for label production is whether to use self-adhesive versus Cheshire labels.[1] If you are putting labels on by hand, only self-adhesive labels are possible. If the labels are to be machine affixed, consult with your mailing coordinator to determine the type of machine to be used for your mailing.

The final consideration for label production is how the materials are to be delivered. If your mailing is to be delivered using the U.S. Postal Service, specify that the sample address labels be run in ZIP code order. This is especially important if your mailing is large, say, 500 pieces or more. The Postal Service will discount postage on large mailings if your addresses are presorted by ZIP code.

If on the odd chance you are dealing with a sample that is not computerized—that is, it does not exist in a machine-readable file—it may well be cost- and time-effective to enter it into a computerized medium.

When entering the address data or setting up the sample file, it is advisable to have the final file accessible to some type of spreadsheet program or other software that will enable you to call up individual respondents on request. If you are going to log in your returns by individual, you will want to be able to call up the identification number of the case and preestablish entry locations for the date of return and the type of outcome. By outcome we mean keeping track of the undeliverables as well as the completes. Examples of outcomes are moved and left no address, no such address, insufficient address, respondent deceased, refused to complete, and completed questionnaire received.

You will want to run sample progress reports at some designated interval, such as once a week. This report should compile the information in your file to document the total number of completed questionnaires, the number of undeliverables, and the number yet to be resolved. These files can be very extensive and can include information on tracking progress variables such as telephone directory search initiated, Department of Motor Vehicles search initiated, search outcome, date of initiation or outcome, and possibly the individual responsible for the search.

In the case of group administration where a sample list is not likely to exist, you will minimally want to keep daily records of number of completes and, if special populations are being sampled, the numbers within each subgroup that have been completed. You should also keep a count of the number of individuals who have declined to participate.

ETHICS AND RESPONSIBILITIES

Always keep respondent confidentiality foremost in your planning. The maintenance and storage of your sample should never provide the opportunity for anyone outside your survey staff to see who, what, and where potential respondents are, nor whether or not they have returned the survey. As is often the case, you may have individuals working on some aspect of your study who have never been exposed to survey research. It is incumbent on you to educate these employees on the protection of subjects and any information that may have been gathered about them.

In some work settings, such as hospitals, clinics, or schools, there may already be established a human subjects protection committee whose mandate is to review all research protocols and ensure that no harm can come to respondents if they participate in any research. Protecting the respondents and doing them no harm are the primary responsibilities of anyone who conducts a survey.

Another "standard" adopted by the sincere surveyor is to be honest about your intent in the survey. It is dishonest to solicit participation in any type of survey under one pretext and then use the survey to promote something else. Some surveyors will claim that they are not trying to solicit a product or money and then turn around and try to sell a product or solicit funds later in the interview. Sometimes, information is solicited in the interview that is later used for a follow-up for solicitation. This is not only deceitful but gives the entire profession of survey research a bad name.

SAMPLE SIZE

Several factors must be taken into account when considering the size or number of individuals or institutions to whom you will administer or send the questionnaire. The first concern should be to determine how many completed responses will be required to demonstrate that your research hypothesis is correct. There are several easy-to-use publications available that provide basic survey sampling guidelines (see **How to Design Surveys** and **How to Sample in Surveys,** Vols. 5 and 6, respectively, in this series). In situations where the number of individuals qualified to respond to your survey is limited, you may need to survey the entire universe of individuals or institutions.

Once the minimally acceptable completed sample size (the number of filled-out, returned questionnaires) has been determined, the total sample size, or the number of individuals or addresses required to produce the desired number of usable returns, can be estimated. With self-administered questionnaires in group settings, sample loss occurs because individuals decline to participate, group turnout is lower than expected, or the materials have not been distributed as directed. In mailed surveys, there are two main causes of respondent loss that need to be compensated for: bad addresses and nonresponse.

If an initial purpose of the mailing is to screen a population for particular characteristics, it will be necessary to factor in the proportion of your overall population that you estimate will qualify and increase your mailing sample size accordingly. For example, you have a list of all homeowners in a particular area, but your primary focus is on homeowners with minor children in the household. You will need to obtain an estimate of the proportion of owner-occupied homes with children under 18 in residence and adjust your overall mailing size upward to account for the loss of owner-occupied homes without minor children.

All address lists are subject to attrition and error. Often, these lists are at least a year old. In some population types, residential or occupational mobility is extremely high. Also, many address files are based on information that is handwritten; therefore, the entry is subject to the interpretation of the individual typing in the data as well as the completeness of the information provided. Typing or entry errors are a final source of address error. It takes only one error in street address or ZIP code to render a mailing undeliverable.

Due to these sources of error, the next item for consideration in determining sample size is an estimate of the proportion of names and/or addresses in your sample file that will be unusable. By unusable we mean those mailings that the post office has deemed undeliverable. Some of the reasons for postal nondelivery are addressee unknown, moved and left no for-warding address, forwarding order has expired, incomplete address, no such address, and refused delivery. The post office will maintain forwarding address orders for one year and no longer. You will need an estimate of the proportion of the sample you will lose for these reasons.

It may be possible for the supplier to estimate the loss based on prior experience, or you may have to conduct a pretest to arrive at this figure. A pretest would involve mailing a packet to a small representative group from the sample to determine the rate of bad returns. Ideally, you will have conducted at least one pilot pretest of your questionnaire and methodology (see Chapter 3). A pilot test of the methods and questionnaire to be used in your final study can provide the rate of bad returns while assessing questionnaire performance.

There are two approaches to compensating for bad addresses. You may decide not to pursue the bad addresses and simply provide enough overage in the sample draw to compensate for these returns, or you may try to track the correct addresses. Usually, no matter how good your tracking efforts, some respondents can never be found. Be aware that by simple replacement of good addresses for bad ones (e.g., not tracking new information on the original sample), you may introduce a level of bias into your results by including only those respondents who are easy to reach or who are either residentially or occupationally less mobile. This can have major consequences, depending on the focus of the research.

The next consideration for estimating sample size is the anticipated response rate, or the number of subjects from the sample population who will complete and return the questionnaire within the study time period. The proportion of respondents who do not participate compared to the number who could have is referred to as the nonresponse rate. Response rates for mailed surveys can vary widely, depending on the accuracy of the sampled addresses, the rigor of the follow-up procedures, the quality of presentation of the study materials, and respondent incentive or interest in the study topic.

Another consideration for the success of a survey, self-administered or mailed, is timing. If at all possible do not initiate surveys around the time of major holidays. Generally, these are times when postal volume increases, and you do not want your survey to risk being delayed or lost in delivery because of the extra load being handled by the postal service at this time. Also, many households and businesses are inundated at these times with charity appeals, mail-order catalogues, and other "pulp" materials. Your survey runs a greater risk of being discarded or put aside during these peak periods. Finally, you will not want your survey conducted at a time when individuals are already overloaded with preparations for a holiday. Depending on the type of individuals being surveyed, summer months when people tend to go on vacation can also be deadly times for response rates.

Other Factors Affecting Response Rates

Mailing experiments have tested hand-addressed envelopes versus typed addresses, typed versus affixed labels, and affixed postage versus postal metering. Some of these treatments have a positive but nonsignificant effect on response rates, but special treatment of the mailing does have a beneficial effect. Accuracy of the sampled addresses has already been discussed; follow-up procedures and respondent motivation are covered later in this chapter. Response rates for mailed surveys can be 30% or lower when follow-up is minimal and the sample is composed of disinterested, nonmotivated respondents. Conversely, when there is repeated contact with respondents by mail and by telephone and a large portion of the respondents are interested and motivated, response rates up to 70% or more have been achieved.

Components of the Field or Mailing Packet

Successfully completing self-administered surveys, especially mailed surveys, requires good coordination and great attention to detail because of the numerous steps involved. The best way to impose organization on a self-administered study is to make a checklist of all the major steps involved. The best way to anticipate the steps involved is to make a checklist of the components of the group administration or mailing packet.

Group Administration Packet Checklist

✓ **Sample: Access and means of selection?**

✓ **Schedule: Calendar of date/time/place**

✓ **Informed consent: If necessary, quantity?**

✓ **Cover letter: Print quantity?**

✓ **Questionnaire: Print quantity?**

✓ **Incentive: If used, quantity?**

✓ **Other handouts: If any, quantity?**

✓ **Means of retrieval: Collect/box/mail back?**

Mailing Packet Checklist

✓ **Sample labels/addresses: Quantity? Number of follow-ups?**

✓ **Outgoing mail envelopes: Quantity? Size of questionnaire? Additional materials? Number of follow-ups?**

✓ **Outgoing postage: Metered or stamped?**

✓ **Cover letter: Print quantity? Initial letter? Follow-up letter(s)?**

✓ **Questionnaire: Print quantity? Number of remailings?**

✓ **Incentive: If used, quantity?**

✓ **Other inserts: If any, quantity?**

✓ **Return mail envelope: Postage-paid business reply/ metered/stamps? Number of remailings?**

Follow-Up Procedures

The surest method for increasing response rates is through follow-ups. By follow-ups we mean recontacting respondents to remind them to complete the questionnaire and mail it back. These follow-ups can be in the form of a postcard, a letter, a telephone call, and/or a complete remailing. Some studies use mailgrams or telegrams or overnight, registered, or certified mail to draw attention to the study and to stress the importance of each return. Minimally, you will want to send a follow-up postcard or letter to either your nonrespondents or the entire sample approximately 10 days after you posted your initial mailing. This postcard or letter should remind respondents that they have been sent a questionnaire to fill out and return, restate the importance of their participation, and encourage them to take a few minutes to do so now if they have not already done so. Include the name and telephone number of someone on the project staff to call collect if the respondent has misplaced the questionnaire and wishes a replacement to be sent, as is shown on the postcard used in the Workplace Assault Study (see Figure 3–7 in Chapter 3).

In this letter or postcard, indicate that you are aware of the possibility that the respondent has already completed and mailed the materials and apologize for any nuisance this follow-up mailing may have caused. Sometimes, offering the respondent an excuse for not responding helps (e.g., "We recognize how busy your schedule must be . . ."; "Perhaps like many of us do when we are busy, you have put the questionnaire to one side and forgotten it . . ."; or "Perhaps someone else in your office/household has mistakenly thrown the questionnaire away"—then explain that all they need to do is call and another packet will be sent). Of course, if you are working with a postcard, the text will have to be brief and all you can accomplish is to ask the respondent to complete the questionnaire and send it back.

Another option is using facsimile (fax) machine transmission. If your respondents have a fax machine or access to one, you can fax them the questionnaire. Conversely, you can encourage respondents to fax their completed forms back to you if they have the means to do so. If the subject matter of the questionnaire is such that it would reveal confidential material, you would not want to suggest this method unless you are able to guarantee that no one outside the project team could possibly see the material.

Depending on the nature and confidentiality of your study, it is desirable to have assigned an unique identification number to each subject in the sample population prior to mailing. This number should be printed somewhere on the questionnaire itself or on the return mail envelope. The back or last page of the questionnaire is the least obtrusive. If you have been explicit about confidentiality in your cover letter that was sent with the questionnaire, few respondents will react negatively to seeing an identification number on their materials. There are always the few exceptions who will scratch out or tear off the identification number.

There are two major reasons for assigning identification numbers before mailing. First, you will be able to keep track of who has responded by logging the returns against a master sample list of the individuals to whom you sent the mailing. Knowing who has not responded allows you to limit your follow-up efforts to only that group of individuals rather than the entire sample. In a large study, you can realize significant savings in the time and cost involved in conducting follow-ups. Second, identifying the sample can sometimes provide you with a profile of the nonresponding group so that you may venture an estimate of how alike or different the two groups are (respondents vs. nonrespondents). Clearly, the more alike they are, the better your data will represent the sampled population.

TYPE, NUMBER, AND TIMING OF FOLLOW-UPS

There are several issues to consider when planning follow-ups for your survey: the type, the number to be conducted, and how frequently or at what critical times to administer them. Typically, these decisions are based on the resources available to you and the amount of time you have allotted for your study. If you are producing a sample status report, as discussed earlier, you will find these reports an invaluable aid in deciding what measures need to be taken for follow-ups.

For example, if from the sample status report you see that after the first follow-up you have received 80% of your expected returns, you may decide to conduct only one more follow-up. If you are collecting data in a group setting and your "completes" are coming in at a faster rate than expected, you may need to alter your sampling interval to collect respondents at a slower rate, or you may want to lower the number of days during which you collect data.

Conversely, if after your first follow-up you have only received 20% of your expected returns, you may decide to conduct more intensive follow-ups, such as telephone calls and priority mailings, sooner than originally anticipated. If, from these reports, you notice a particularly high rate of bad addresses—that is, the number of nondeliverables precludes your ability to obtain the minimally desired number of returns from your study—you may want to pursue the possibility of pulling another sample. In a group administration, if the number of "completes" is lower than anticipated, you may shorten the sampling interval, add more days to the administration, or add more sites of administration.

Mailed follow-ups require additional printing, postage, envelopes, and labor. Telephone follow-ups assume that you have valid telephone numbers for your respondents and require considerable labor and the space and equipment to conduct the telephone calls, which may involve toll or long-distance charges besides the monthly cost of the telephone. Depending on the type of sample you are seeking, numerous calls may be required to contact each respondent. This is particularly true with elite samples, such as doctors, public figures, and executives.

As mentioned earlier, conducting follow-ups is the best means of increasing response rate. At minimum, you will want to send a postcard reminder to each person in your sample who has not returned a completed questionnaire. Typically, this postcard is sent 10 days to 2 weeks after the initial mailing date, with subsequent follow-ups made at 2-week intervals or longer.

If you have the time and resources to conduct several follow-ups of various types, it is often best to begin with the least expensive method first—postcard or letter—and use more expensive methods later, such as a complete remailing of the packet, priority mailings (e.g., registered or certified letter, mailgrams, etc.), and telephone calls. If you have been able to keep a log of your sample returns and can identify who has not responded, you will be using the more expensive methods on increasingly smaller sample sizes. Although this is a more economical approach, the researcher does not always have the luxury of time to consider this.

The greatest efficiency for follow-ups seems to peak at about three or four. Obviously, if time and money are of no consequence you may make as many attempts as you wish. There does come a point, however, at which it makes no sense and is in fact no longer relevant to push for returns. This is a highly individual decision. If response has been particularly poor on a study, some researchers will continue to make follow-up attempts using every resource available. Remember, the credibility of the study rests in large part on the number of sampled individuals you have successfully represented.

When the telephone is used as a follow-up method, it is not uncommon for the call to be used as a means of gathering the data contained in the questionnaire rather than waiting for a mailed response. This assumes that the individuals making the calls are familiar with telephone interviewing and with the questionnaire and are capable of collecting the data in a competent manner. A telephone interview is only possible when the questionnaire you are using is relatively brief and does not require the respondent to have access to other information, such as files or records, to answer the questions. In studies where self-administration is the only desirable method due to study sensitivity or the perceived honesty of the respondent, you will not want to use the telephone to collect the data.

If you do collect some of your data using the telephone, it is wise to indicate in the data set which interviews have been self-administered and which were conducted by telephone. In survey jargon, this is known as using "mixed methodologies." It has been established that the various modes of administration—face-to-face, telephone, self-administered—have different effects on the respondent and hence on the data. When you begin analyzing your data you should compare the results found with each of the modes of administration to ensure that the distribution of answers across questions is not dramatically different. If gross differences are found, you may decide to report the information from the two methods separately or combine the two but report your findings with a caveat about possible unreliability of the data, or you may decide not to use the data obtained by a method different from that by which the majority was collected.

When using self-administered questionnaires in a group setting there is often little that can be done to follow up on those individuals who were not present at the time of administration. If the study is being conducted in a more structured setting, such as a classroom, clinic, or place of work, it is possible to keep track of all individuals in attendance at the time of administration. In this case, it is possible to approach these individuals either at another visit or through another individual (e.g., a teacher, supervisor, or nurse) who has contact with these people, or you may be able to contact them by telephone.

In deciding to make follow-up contacts, you want to consider whether there is a risk of "contaminating" the data in that the nonrespondents may have had the opportunity to discuss the contents of the survey with those who were present at the time of administration and therefore may respond to the survey differently from how they would have if they had answered without prior knowledge. In the situation where a self-administered questionnaire is being brought to the sampled individual, such as schoolchildren bringing a questionnaire home for a parent to complete, the same courier—in this case, the student—can take reminders to the respondent.

CONTENT OF THE FOLLOW-UP REMINDER

The wording of the follow-up communication is similar to the initial cover letter sent with the first mailing. If a postcard is being used, it could be worded as simply as this:

> A few weeks ago you received a questionnaire from (name of sponsor/researcher/organization) asking for your participation in a very important study about (topic). To date we have not received your response. It is very important that we be able to include your opinions in our study. If you have already responded, thank you for your help and excuse this card. If you have not responded, won't you please take a minute now to do so? If you require additional information, please call (contact person and telephone number) collect. Again, thank you.

If you are using a letter, you can expand on the importance of the study and its purpose or use. Make a point to explain how important the respondent is to the success of your study and mention that he or she is one of a select few who have been picked to represent hundreds or thousands of others, depending on the universe from which the sample was drawn. Reinforce that the data are confidential and that the individual will not be identified in any way. If you have the endorsement or sponsorship of an individual or organization known to the respondent, indicate their support of the study. Finally, provide a name and telephone number where the individual may call for more information or another packet to be sent.

If the telephone is being used to make follow-up calls, select the individuals making the calls carefully. Callers should have pleasant, friendly voices. Unless you are dealing with a non-English-speaking population, you will want callers with speaking patterns similar to those of your sample. If reminder calls are made by individuals with heavy accents, the respondent may become frustrated trying to understand the caller and possibly will become alienated from your study.

All callers should work from a script. A script is essentially a written structure not unlike the follow-up letter. Callers should identify themselves, their affiliation, and the purpose of the call. Again, the importance of the study and the respondent's participation should be the focus. This script should contain all the information the caller will need to answer any questions a respondent might have. Although each caller develops an individual style for effectiveness, a script helps prevent your caller from creating dialogue on the spot or giving information to the respondent that may be misleading or untrue. In some cases, it may be necessary for a higher-level supervisor or even the researcher to speak on the telephone with a reluctant respondent.

If you decide to use the telephone to gather data from the individuals you successfully contact, pretest the questionnaire a few times over the telephone to make sure that it will adapt well to telephone administration. There are some types of self-administered questions that do not lend themselves well to telephone interviewing and may need to be modified in some way. This is another reason to record which interviews were conducted via telephone versus self-administration. Changing the format of the question can produce dramatically different results.

If you are conducting multiple follow-ups, it is profitable to keep track of the response rate after each method is tried. For example, if your first follow-up is a postcard, note how many returns come in after the card is sent and before the next method is used. Say the next method you use is a remailing of all the study materials. You might mark the questionnaires that go out in this mailing with an identifiable mark so that when they are returned you can differentiate the returns between the first mailing and this follow-up. Keep track of the effect of each procedure. If you should happen to conduct another mailed survey in the future, you can better judge how many and which follow-ups give the best return for the invest-ment. It is possible you will even have to use this information later in your first study. If your goal is to get as many returns as is humanly possible, you may want to evaluate which method or methods worked best with your sample population and try it or them again.

Whether postcards, letters, or telephone calls, follow-up attempts are extremely important to the overall success of the study. Because they are so important, do not treat these pro-cedures casually. Method of delivery, content, and quality of presentation all leave an impression on the potential respon-dent. You will witness the rewards for your efforts by the level of response you receive.

Follow-Up Procedure Guidelines

- Ten days after original mailing, send follow-up.
- Follow-up can be a postcard, letter, or telephone call.
- Use a mailgram or telegram or overnight, registered, or certified mail to call more attention to the survey mailing.
- Use a facsimile machine for sending and/or receiving questionnaires.
- Content of follow-up message should stress the importance of response and purpose of study.
- Include in the text of letter the name and telephone number of a survey staff member who can be contacted for assistance in responding.
- Conduct additional follow-ups every 10 days.
- Keep track of the rate of return for each follow-up method used.

SAMPLE TRACKING

There are two basic types of mailing addresses: residential and commercial. In designing the study you will have decided whether the sample target is a particular individual, an address, or a position. In other words, do you want Jane Doe at 111 Main Street, or is any adult living at 111 Main Street appropriate?

Another example is whether you want John Smith, Employee Benefits Manager for Company XYZ, or whoever is filling the position of Employee Benefits Manager at XYZ. If your mailed packet is returned because the specific individual cited is no longer there, you do not need to track the address; simply change the name or make the addressee noncommittal, such as "Resident" or "Employee Benefits Manager." Ideally, you will have set the address file up this way at the onset of the work so that this becomes an issue only in a rare event.

When the focal point of a mailing is a specific individual, tracking becomes essential. In the case of bad addresses or unknown addressees, the Postal Service will not automatically notify you of such outcomes. If an addressee has moved and the mail forwarding order (which the post office retains for one year only and then destroys) is active, the mailing packet will automatically be sent to the new address without your being given the updated address. If a packet is undeliverable due to a bad address, no such person, or other condition, it often remains in a "dead letter" bin at the post office without your knowledge.

It is a wise idea to have made a rubber stamp saying "ADDRESS CORRECTION REQUESTED—DO NOT FOR-WARD" to stamp on each outgoing mailing packet or, if you use an envelope addressing system, to program this into the address. The Postal Service will charge you 50¢ for each address correction, but by using this procedure you will retain better control of the sample.

Bad addresses can also occur through human error. If an envelope is returned with a notation of "no such address," "no such number," or "no such street," some common sense and a quick check of a local street guide may clear up the problem. It could be that the street name was misspelled, that the street needs a direction such as north, south, east, or west, or that the ZIP code is wrong.

Changes of addresses should be corrected or updated and remailed. Updates of corrected or new addresses should be made to the sample files for future follow-up contact. If the new or correct address for an individual is not found, tracking of respondents can be initiated if time and budget allow.

There are numerous resources that can be used in attempting to obtain correct respondent addresses. The process of trying to find out where an individual has gone is sometimes referred to as tracking. The first place to look for updates is the sample supplier. It is possible that the provider may have new addresses or address corrections for sampled respondents that have not yet been changed in the main data file.

Typically, even if the supplier is able to provide some corrections, there will still be those addresses that are unresolved. Business addresses are typically easier to track than are those for individuals. If the business is local, it may be as simple as looking in the telephone directory, checking both residential and classified listings. Calling the local telephone company's directory information may be another resource, especially if the institution has recently moved. Reverse directories, also called cross-reference or criss-cross directories, are telephone directories that are referenced by city, street name and number, and telephone number. These are also useful for tracking. There are several major companies that publish these directories. Criss-cross directories may also be found in your public library or at your local telephone company headquarters.

Many marketing companies and/or directory publishers maintain address files for the majority of mailing addresses in the United States and often can provide certain types of samples. They can produce mailing labels, and some will fold, stuff, seal, and post your mailing for you for a price.

As the geographic area of the sample gets wider, the number of resources required to track sample addresses gets more complex. Typically, most institutions maintain only their local directories. It is not unusual for a major public library to keep telephone directories for other major metropolitan areas. Your local telephone company headquarters may maintain a reference library of all the telephone directories produced by the parent company. If the number of addresses to be checked is large, it may be worthwhile to pay a directory publishing company to run these checks for you against their computer database.

The ability to access information about a particular individual varies widely across areas in the United States. In some states, the Department of Motor Vehicles will allow a search of drivers' licenses, usually for a fee. Other states, like California, require special permission to search without permission from the individual license holder. In any case, having the name, date of birth, and last known address of the individual you are tracking can help narrow down the possibilities.

Another option involves local public utilities, such as gas, water, and electricity. Regulations on obtaining this type of information vary considerably from area to area. Public utilities and other resources in large metropolitan areas are less likely to provide information on individuals than are those located in less populated areas.

Sample Tracking Procedure Guidelines

- Check for typographical or clerical errors in address.
- Remail new packet to each corrected address.
- Stamp outgoing envelopes "ADDRESS CORRECTION REQUESTED" and correct address file based on corrected returns.
- Remail to corrected addresses.
- Check with sample provider for updates, if applicable.

- Check telephone directories, telephone directory information, and reverse directories.
- Check utilities/Department of Motor Vehicles.

Processing Returns

Having a plan for the handling of returns is as important as collecting the data. When we write of processing the returns we mean the methods used to record the receipt of the completed questionnaires and how the data from these instruments will be converted into numeric results ready for analysis. It is assumed that these returns will be entered into a computer file and read into some software that can be used to compile the results and hopefully calculate at least basic statistics on the findings. Some self-administered surveys are processed or analyzed by hand rather than on a computer, so most of the processing procedures discussed in this section pertain to both hand and computer tabulation.

SAMPLE STATUS REPORTS

Earlier in the section entitled "Preparing the Sample," we discussed the merits of maintaining a sample log or roster, either in paper-pencil form or computerized, to check-in your returns. Ideally, this log will reflect the identification number assigned to the respondent; number and types of follow-ups; tracking procedures used, if any; corrections to the mailing file, if any; and the date the completed questionnaire was received. In organizations that routinely conduct surveys, the next item in this file might be a date indicating when a questionnaire is turned over to data reduction. The ideal sample log is a means by which the location and status of any given questionnaire can be found upon request.

DATA REDUCTION ·

Data reduction may include the editing of the completed questionnaires, coding of any open-ended material, providing codes for missing data, eliminating incorrect responses, and entering the questionnaire responses into a machine-readable file. In some organizations, data may still be keypunched onto an 80-column card and read into a computer, but in most instances, the data are entered directly onto the hard drive or onto a diskette. In more technologically advanced settings, the data may be entered into the data file via scanning. Numerous software programs are available for setting up a data entry format that is analyzable by statistical software or spreadsheet programs.

Returned questionnaires should not go to data entry without prior editing. Respondents may have skipped questions or entire sections of the questionnaire. In questions asking for only one answer, respondents may have recorded several. Questions that were inappropriate for the respondent to answer, based on some prior information elicited, may have been answered. The respondent may have felt that the answer categories given were insufficient and decided to write an alternative answer on the page. Perhaps the handwriting is barely legible. The ways that individuals can find for not following instructions (no matter how straightforward the instructions nor how simple the questions) are as varied and numerous as are the differences between and among people. As a result, you should plan on having someone edit or look over each completed questionnaire prior to data entry.

How these inconsistencies or inaccuracies are handled is at the discretion of the researcher. If the correct response is obvious, the researcher may allow corrections to be made. In some cases, where respondent telephone numbers are available, the respondent may be called to clarify or obtain the response on the questionnaire. In other cases where a problem answer has occurred, no response may be taken. In any case, a plan will have to be developed whereby inconsistent, incorrect, or missing data are either assigned a numeric value or skipped altogether.

Who handles this varies. In some survey houses, the questionnaires are edited by field clerks in an area that specializes in the collection of data. In other places, the questionnaires are edited as part of the coding process. Coding is the process of converting written answers into numerics using an established coding scheme or plan. This plan is known as a codebook. A coding clerk may edit and code the instrument in one step. In some research houses, the editing, coding, and data entry are performed concomitantly. It is our opinion that this places too great a burden on the individual and invites error. If the same person is to perform all tasks it would be better to have editing and coding done in one step and the data entry done separately. (More in-depth instruction on the processing of data is found in Bourque and Clark's *Processing Data,* which is listed in the Suggested Readings section at the end of this book.)

Estimating Costs

Typically, you will be required to develop an estimate of costs to conduct a self-administered or mailed survey prior to the time you actually incur expenses. The first decision you must make prior to estimating costs is sample size. Specifically, you will need to know how many initial mailings you anticipate, an estimate of the number of completed returns you expect, and costs for address corrections if you plan to use this option.

In the following pages, we first cover expenses unique to a mailed survey, then costs that are unique to a self-administered study, and finally, costs that occur with either method.

There are two types of costs: out-of-pocket expenses and constant costs, or costs for labor that is expended whether or not the study is conducted. Out-of-pocket expenses are those that you must pay for; that is, they are costs for items not routinely paid for by your organization. Such costs might include postage, printing, envelopes, incentives, and any labor required for tasks that are not covered by employees already paid for. An example of a labor cost is the use of a mailing company to fold, stuff, and affix labels and postage to your mailing.

A word of caution: The expenditures itemized in the subsequent sections are approximate costs for January 1995. Certain costs listed may fluctuate considerably with geographic region. Labor charges that are inherent in certain items vary by location. Other overhead costs or markups similarly vary by the expense of doing business in different areas. Finally, the price of stock materials, such as envelopes or paper, may decrease, depending on the volume in which they are purchased. Generally, costs go down as volume increases. The dollar amounts presented here are meant as guidelines only—it is up to the individual surveyor to seek out the appropriate costs for these items in his or her market area.

OUTGOING POSTAGE

For a mailed study, you will need a postal scale that can accurately weigh ounces so you can estimate postage expense. Postal scales are commonly found in most office settings. Assemble a packet that mimics what you plan to send. For example, you will need an outgoing mail envelope, a return mail envelope, a sheet of paper to represent the cover letter, the questionnaire (use the number of pages you anticipate for the final copy), the incentive, if you plan to offer one, and other materials you plan to include in this mailing. Weighing all these materials together on the scale will tell you how many ounces the outgoing packet weighs.

Using the same packet, remove the cover letter, outgoing envelope, incentive, and any materials other than the return mail envelope and questionnaire and/or any other materials to be sent back by the respondent and then calculate the weight in ounces of the return mail packet. This will tell you the amount of postage required to return the packet to you. The cost of providing return-mail postage is discussed later in this section.

Always send materials at the first-class postage rate. Second-, third-, fourth-class, or other bulk-rate postage sends the message that the study and the respondent are not important to you. As of January 1, 1995 the typical outgoing postage is 32¢ for the first ounce and 23¢ for each additional ounce or fraction of an ounce. The post office offers discounts off this rate for mailings of 500 pieces or more that are presorted by ZIP code. To qualify for this discount, you must have at least 10 pieces outgoing to each ZIP code in your mailing. If you can meet these requirements, the discount rate is 27.4¢ per ounce. There are other cost breaks for mailings that use ZIP+4 or barcodes. It is wise to inquire about Postal Service rates and requirements before making a cost estimate and setting up your sample specifications.

You also need to include the cost of follow-up postage, if any, when preparing your estimate. Postcard postage is currently 20¢. The Postal Service sells sheets of 40 cards for $8.00 each. Again, there are discounts for presorting using ZIP+4 and barcoding. If a letter is to be sent as a reminder, assume it will be one ounce at 32¢. You can also buy personalized stamped envelopes from the Postal Service for $176.40 per 500 #10 envelopes. The decision to use stamped envelopes from the Postal Service should be based on resource availability.

If you work in a setting where there is a clerk to meter the postage, you may not need to buy prestamped envelopes. Similarly, if you can get a better volume discount on printing personalized envelopes or if such envelopes are freely available to you at your place of work, it makes no monetary sense to purchase prestamped envelopes. If you intend to remail the entire study packet at some point, the postage will be the same per-piece cost as in your original mailing.

INCOMING POSTAGE

You must include a self-addressed business reply envelope with the mailing. There are two options for providing return-mail postage: Affix sufficient postage in the form of stamps to the return envelope or open a postage-paid business reply mail account (BRM) with your post office. Affixing postage can be a waste of money in that not all respondents will complete and return the questionnaire. In these cases, you have spent the money for the postage but have not received a return. The postage-paid business reply option costs more than the regular per-ounce postal rate because there is an $85.00 12-month permit fee plus a surcharge for the handling. If the mailing is large enough the savings from using BRM more than offsets the loss of providing postage in the mailing.

There are two surcharge rates for BRM handling. If your expected return is fewer than 600 pieces, the post office will not require a deposit to open an account for handling returns, but the additional charge per piece over and above the postage is 44¢. If your expected return is more than 600 pieces, you can establish a BRM account with a minimum deposit of $205.00; then the handling surcharge is 10¢ per piece.

OPTIONAL MAILINGS

Charges for special handling by the postal service include Return Receipt Requested at the time of mailing, showing who signed for the packet and on what date, at $1.10, special delivery at $9.95, registered mail at $4.85, Express Mail next-day at $10.75, or certified mail at $1.10. Other delivery options are Federal Express, United Parcel Service, and other parcel delivery services. Although these options are more expensive, they do draw attention to the study and communicate its importance. Although budgetary constraints are always a consideration, the trade-off involved in paying for postage that enhances the quality presentation of the study materials versus saving a few dollars may not be worth the savings if a low response rate makes the study unusable.

PRINTED AND STOCK MATERIALS

The next budget item for consideration is the cost of printed materials used for the study. Some of these items may already be available to you without special purchasing, such as outgoing envelopes; others will not be. It is assumed that your materials for printing will be camera-ready. That is, you will have typed or word processed the final products as they will appear in print. Your printer will either film the originals and create a negative for printing or use a duplicating process, such as a photocopier. The quality of duplication today is such that on some machines you can barely tell a difference between the printer's page and a copier-generated one.

If your mailing is not bulky, you may be able to use a #11 (4½″ × 10⅜″) envelope for your outgoing packet and a #10 (4⅛″ × 9½″) envelope for returning the completed questionnaire. "Not bulky" means that your questionnaire is brief, no more than one 11″ × 17″ page folded and printed front and back, resulting in four printed sides, that your cover letter is one page, that you use a #10 reply envelope, and that there are no additional inserts to the mailing. The cost of 500 nonpersonalized #11 envelopes is approximately $27.00, and for similar #10s, $16.00.

Larger mailings will require the use of manilla-type envelopes. Not only can you put thicker materials into these envelopes, your materials do not have to be prefolded before being stuffed into the envelope. Heavy-duty 10″ × 13″, self-sealing, white first-class envelopes cost approximately $142.00 per 500. You will include in your mailing packet the same type of envelope for returning the questionnaire but it will be smaller (9″ × 12″) and costs about the same.

The outgoing envelopes should have your project name, organization name, and address imprinted in the upper left-hand corner or sender section of the incoming envelope. Incoming envelopes must have your business address in the addressee section in the middle of the front of the envelope. You may also want to repeat your address in the sender section of the envelope.

If a fairly high volume of mail is received at the return address you are using, you will want to identify your project on the face of the envelope either in the lower left-hand side or as a line in the addressee section. This will help the mail sorter identify your packets and deliver them in a timely fashion. If you are using barcoding, you will also need to print this on your return-mail envelope.

You should allow approximately 4¢ per piece for imprinting addresses. Due to high volume, it is possible that your printer will be able to bid the printing job, including the cost for envelopes, at a rate lower than you would get if you bought them separately. Again, when costing your study, remember to include the cost for additional follow-up mailing envelopes.

Other items that will be printed are the cover letter and the questionnaire. Printing costs for 500 letters on 20-pound bond paper will be approximately $25.00. Five hundred copies of a questionnaire printed on one piece of 11″ × 17″ paper on four sides and folded will cost about $125.00. The cost per printed side comes out to about 6.25¢ per printed side. Not only will these costs fluctuate from area to area due to varying labor and overhead costs, they will also vary depending on the weight and type of paper used for printing and the means by which the questionnaires are bound. When printing questionnaires on the front and back of the page, it is better to use 60-pound paper to eliminate the possibility of print "bleeding" through to the other side.

Always overprint the number of items you need. In other words, if you are mailing to 500 respondents, you should print 600 copies. These additional copies can be used to document the questionnaire in your archival files, to distribute to other workers or supervisors, to have on hand if some of the printing is unusable, and to replace any that might get lost or damaged.

Before you release materials for printing, decide whether or not you plan a second complete mailing to your sample. If so, it is more economical to print all the questionnaires at one time. Volume reduces cost per piece, plus you are not paying two separate job-setup fees. Always allow sufficient time before your mailing date for the printing to be done. If you are on an extremely tight time schedule, your printer will charge extra for "rush" printing. When estimating printing costs, remember to include the cost of printing follow-up letters or other materials you may use.

If you plan to use an incentive, the cost obviously will be dependent on the gift. Small key chains can be purchased for about 25¢ each, retractable ballpoint pens for around 50¢ each, or you may elect to enclose a $1 bill in the mailing (make sure that you send new, clean bills). You can estimate the most you would spend on an incentive and multiply that cost by the sample size to get a figure for your cost estimate. If you plan to include other materials in your mailing, you will need to add the cost for this into your budget.

Personnel Requirements

Material expenses are but one part of the cost to conduct a study. There is also a considerable amount of labor involved. Mailed studies generally require more labor than do self-administered studies simply because there are a great many tasks to be performed that require considerable coordination and management. Much of the labor needed to conduct these studies is at the skilled clerical level, but you will want the person coordinating the project to have the following charac-teristics: creative, detail oriented, good at managing tasks and individuals, good at problem solving, resourceful, skilled in communicating with vendors and other employees, and using good logic. It would be advantageous if the project manager had some degree of experience with word processing and spreadsheet programs on the personal computer. Ultimately, you will need at least one person with these skills so that you can produce your camera-ready copy of the questionnaire and set up a computerized record-keeping system for sample track-ing. Also, prior experience obtaining bids for supplies and printing would be very helpful.

These same characteristics apply to the individual who man-ages a study requiring data collection by self-administration. It will be this person's responsibility to coordinate the printing and gathering of materials necessary to conduct the admini-stration, to get cooperation from the sites to be included, to set up the logistics of date and time and availability of the desired population, to provide the trained individuals who will go to these sites to distribute and collect the forms if appropriate, and to see to the processing of the completed questionnaires as they are returned.

You may decide to contract out the labor-intensive aspects of your study: folding the study materials and stuffing them into the outgoing envelopes, affixing the address labels, opening up the returns as they come in, editing and coding the completed questionnaires, and entering the data into a computer file. Companies that provide mailing services—that is, they fold, stuff, label, and post your materials—can be found nearly everywhere as data processing companies that will open the envelopes, edit and code them according to your specifications, and then enter them into a file for you. If no tabulating experts or facilities are available within your organization, most data processing companies will also process your data, provide you with frequency distributions (the count and percentage of the number of responses to each answer category in a question) of your data, and cross-tabulate data to your specifications.

If you are able to perform this work within your organization, you will need to have one or more clerical workers, depending on the size of the study. The clerical workers needed on a mailed survey must be good with detail and work well with numbers. One or a few of the clerks, depending on the volume of work, should have some word processing and/or spreadsheet experience, and at least one should have 10-key experience for data entry.

For a self-administered study, you may need clerical-level help to carry out the survey administration. These will be the individuals who go to each study location and monitor and distribute the questionnaires to be completed. Depending on the complexity of the study, these individuals may have to conduct on-the-spot sampling, make random respondent selections, make oral presentations regarding the purpose of the study and its sponsorship, and finally, be able to answer questions about any particular item in the questionnaire or about the study in general. These individuals should be selected for their ability to interact with others and to present themselves with a sense of competence and authority.

Unfortunately, the effort required to conduct either a mailed or self-administered study is not constant over the duration of the project. There are times of heavy labor intensity and then times during which little or no effort is required. It is best if the management personnel required for this project are already in place and can allocate time to running the study.

The clerical time required is not as much of a problem. If clerical personnel are not routinely available in your setting, it is usually not difficult to find part-time, hourly workers from temporary personnel agencies. If you are located near a college or university, students can be a rich source of clerical help. There is a wide variance in the hourly wage for clerical workers, depending on geographic location and the level of skills required. Clerks who will fold, stuff, and affix labels need not be as skilled as those who will edit, code, and use personal computers. The hourly wage may be as low as $6.00 or as high as $16.00 for these workers.

To determine the number of clerical hours necessary to complete your project, use the following guidelines for a mailed survey using a questionnaire with four open-ended questions and the rest precoded—that is, one 11″ × 17″ sheet folded in half (four printed sides), a #11 outgoing envelope, a #10 return-mail envelope, and a cover letter:

Task	Time
Folding survey materials, stuffing into envelopes, affixing labels to envelopes	100 packets/hour
Postal metering	500/hour
Open envelopes and log return	120 envelopes/hour
Edit a 4-page questionnaire	30 questionnaires/hour
Code 4 questions	12 questionnaires/hour
Enter into a computer file 4 pages/30 questions	30 questionnaires/hour

These figures are based on the assumption that the clerical personnel employed have a familiarity with some of their functions—for example, that data entry personnel are proficient on 10-key pads.

If this survey were to be mailed to 500 individuals, we would budget for 5 hours to fold the materials, stuff them into the envelope, and affix the mailing labels. If you need to add in the cost of metering the envelopes through the postal meter, add another hour to the clerical time.

For the purpose of this exercise, let us assume a response rate of 80%, or 400 returned, completed questionnaires. It would require approximately 4 hours to open the envelopes and check in each one by identification number against the master roster or log, 14 hours to edit these questionnaires, 34 hours to code them, and another 14 hours to enter them into the computer data file.

All told, 72 hours of clerical time are needed to ready the packets for mailing, meter them, log in the returns, edit and code the questionnaires, and enter them into a data file. In your time estimates, you will want to inflate these figures to account for break time, lunch time, and occasional pauses. Although the editing, coding, and data entry can be held and done together and the clerical functions are done all at one time, the logging in of returns must be done piecemeal as they come in so that you can keep track of your sample and response rate and, if necessary, take corrective measures.

The following budget illustrates how to use the costing estimates presented earlier and represents costs to date for the Workplace Assault Study cited throughout this book.

Development of Project	$ Cost
Writing proposal: 4 days @ $362.50/day (senior author's UCLA salary rate/outside consulting rate would double)	1,450.00
First draft of questionnaire and specifications: 2 days @ $362.50/day (senior author's UCLA salary rate)	725.00
Finalizing questionnaire: 8 hours @ $14.94 (project coordinator's hourly rate)	119.52
Establishing contacts and meeting with union personnel: 15 hours @ $14.94	224.10
Organizing and conducting focus groups: 24 hours @ $14.94/hour	358.56
Pretesting questionnaire: 8 hours @ $14.94/hour	119.52
Miscellaneous administrative tasks (arranging meetings, clerical, etc.): 4 hours @ $14.94	59.76
TOTAL DEVELOPMENT COSTS	3,056.46
Mailings	
Purchase and printing of 4 sets of mailing labels (labor contributed by Service Employees International Union [SEIU])	160.00
Purchase of envelopes for advance letter and first mailing of questionnaire	627.00

Development of Project	$ Cost
Advance Letter	
Duplication of 1,800 letters @ 4¢/letter	72.00
Postage for 1,800 letters @ 32¢/letter	576.00
Labor associated with mailing letters contributed by SEIU	
First Mailing of Questionnaire	
Duplication of 1,800 flyers @ 4¢/flyer	72.00
Duplication of 1,800 cover letters @ 4¢/letter	72.00
Duplication of 1,800 22-page questionnaires @ 5¢/page	1,980.00
Postage to mail first questionnaire to 1,744 SEIU members @ $1.01/packet (SEIU provided metering service, and labor to mail each packet)	1,761.44
Postage for 1,744 respondents to mail back first questionnaire @ 78¢/questionnaire (stamps placed on each return envelope)	1,360.32
Collation of 1,744 mailing packets: 54 hours @ $14.94/hour	806.76
TOTAL COST OF MAILING OF FIRST QUESTIONNAIRE	7,487.52
COST PER QUESTIONNAIRE MAILED	4.16
COST PER QUESTIONNAIRE RETURNED ($n = 310$)	24.15
Postcards	
Purchase of 1,800 postcards @ 20¢/card through UCLA + 20% per postcard	432.00
Labor to print postcards contributed by SEIU	
Labor to put labels on postcards: 4 hours @ $14.94/hour	59.76
TOTAL COST OF MAILING POSTCARDS	491.76
ADDITIONAL COST PER RESPONDENT	0.27
COST PER ADDITIONAL RESPONSE OBTAINED ($n = 258$)	1.91
COST PER TOTAL RESPONSE OBTAINED ([$7,487.52 + $491.76]/568)	14.05
Second Mailing of Questionnaire	
Duplication of 1,143 cover letters @ 4¢/letter	45.72
Duplication of 1,143 22-page questionnaires @ 5¢/page	1,257.30

→

Development of Project	$ Cost
Purchase of 3 boxes of 10 × 13 envelopes through UCLA: 500 envelopes/box @ $142.00/box	426.00
Printing of 1,500 envelopes @ 4¢/envelope	60.00
Postage for 1,143 packets through UCLA: 91¢ + 20% per packet	1,248.16
Postage paid on only those returned through UCLA business reply: 78¢ + 44¢ handling + 20% per questionnaire (estimated at n = 304)	445.06
Collation of 1,143 mailing packets: 36 hours @ $14.94/hour	537.84
TOTAL COST OF SECOND FULL MAILING	4,020.08
COST PER ADDITIONAL QUESTIONNAIRE OBTAINED (n = 304)	13.22
COST PER TOTAL RESPONSE OBTAINED ([$7,487.52 + $491.76 + $4,020.08]/872)	13.76
Logging In Returned Questionnaires	
Seven hours @ $14.94/hour for 872 returned questionnaires	104.72
Costs of telephone follow-up on remaining 871 respondents, data entry, and data analysis not available at time of writing	
Supervisory time by senior author over mailings and data entry contributed and not included in total costs	

Although some of the wage rates may not be applicable for your situation, this budget gives a general idea of the materials and personnel requirements needed to conduct a mailed survey. This budget also introduces the idea that some costs can be shared or eliminated by working with other individuals or groups who hold a common interest in the research. Obviously, the more you are able to offset costs within your organization, the less the out-of-pocket expense.

A common error made in first-time mail surveys is in not providing enough resources to cover additional follow-ups if they become necessary. Even though you may have conducted a reasonable pilot test of the procedures and sample, there is always the possibility, as we saw in the union employees sample cited in Chapter 2, that pilot-test returns will not accurately reflect the total population returns for reasons not obvious at the time of planning.

Always have a contingency plan for what you will do if completed returns fall significantly short of the necessary sample goal. It would be a terrible loss to go through all the work required to conduct a survey only to find out that you have insufficient numbers of returns to make use of the data.

Note

1. Cheshire labels are the forerunner to today's self-adhesive labels. Cheshires typically are printed on 8½" × 11" perforated sheets, such that labels are created when the perforations are ripped. The back of each sheet is preglued and requires moisture to affix. Typically, the sheets are run through a machine that chops and moistens each label and then affixes it to an envelope or other materials requiring labeling. Cheshire labels are less expensive than the more commonly used self-adhesive labels.

Exercises

1. A large corporation is considering changing the kinds of health insurance plans made available to their managerial and professional employees. They want to find out the kind of health insurance plans that employees currently have, both through the company and through other sources, and the extent to which employees express interest in three new plans currently under discussion by the corporation. Would a self-administered questionnaire be appropriate for this study, and if so, which type of self-administered questionnaire would you recommend using?

   One-to-one self-administered questionnaire 1
   Group-administered questionnaire 2
   Semisupervised questionnaire passed out in the
       workplace 3
   Questionnaire mailed to employees' homes 4
   Do not use a self-administered questionnaire 5

2. The Parent-Teacher Association (PTA) of an elementary school wants to find out the number of active PTA members who think it would be a good idea to hold a carnival to raise money for extra computer software for the school *and* would be willing to help organize the carnival. Would a self-administered questionnaire be appropriate for this study, and if so, which <u>type</u> of self-administered questionnaire would you recommend using?

```
One-to-one self-administered questionnaire . . . .   1
Group-administered questionnaire . . . . . . . . .   2
Semisupervised questionnaire passed out as
      people come into a PTA meeting  . . . . . . .   3
Semisupervised questionnaire passed out as
      people leave a PTA meeting . . . . . . . . . .   4
Questionnaire mailed to students' homes  . . . . .   5
Do not use a self-administered questionnaire  . . .   6
```

3. A neighborhood association is aware that a number of elderly Russian immigrants have moved into their community. It is their observation that many of these people are afraid to come out of their apartments. They want to find out what they can do to help these new residents of the community. Would a self-administered questionnaire be appropriate for this study, and if so, which <u>type</u> of self-administered questionnaire would you recommend using?

```
One-to-one self-administered questionnaire . . . .   1
Group-administered questionnaire . . . . . . . . .   2
Semisupervised questionnaire distributed at
      community meetings . . . . . . . . . . . . . .   3
Questionnaire mailed to residents' homes . . . . .   4
Do not use a self-administered questionnaire  . . .   5
```

4. A dental clinic located in a university dental school wants to find out how satisfied patients are with their services. They have a draft questionnaire that they need to test to see if it is complete and to find out whether patients can fill it out. Would a self-administered questionnaire be appropriate for this study, and if so, which <u>type</u> of self-administered questionnaire would you recommend using?

> One-to-one self-administered questionnaire 1
> Group-administered questionnaire 2
> Semisupervised questionnaire 3
> Questionnaire mailed to patients' homes 4
> Do not use a self-administered questionnaire 5

5. The management of a factory that manufactures ball bearings has received a lot of complaints from employees about the homeless persons in the area around the factory. The managers have not seen many homeless in the area. They want to find out whether the complaints are representative of the total population of workers in the factory or simply represent the opinions of a few "squeaky wheels." Would a self-administered questionnaire be appropriate for this study, and if so, which <u>type</u> of self-administered questionnaire would you recommend using?

> One-to-one self-administered questionnaire 1
> Group-administered questionnaire 2
> Semisupervised questionnaire passed out as
>   workers punch in for work 3
> Semisupervised questionnaire passed out as
>   workers punch out from work 4
> Questionnaire mailed to workers' homes 5
> Do not use a self-administered questionnaire 6

6. The board of a regional symphony orchestra has received $20,000 from the county government to find out whether county residents know about the symphony, whether they have ever attended a concert, and the kind of music they prefer listening to. Would a self-administered questionnaire be appropriate for this study, and if so, which <u>type</u> of self-administered questionnaire would you recommend using?

One-to-one self-administered questionnaire 1
Questionnaires administered at various group
    meetings 2
Semisupervised questionnaire passed out as
    people come into community meetings 3
Semisupervised questionnaire passed out as
    people leave various community meetings . . . 4
Questionnaire mailed to a sample of 500 county
    residential addresses 5
Do not use a self-administered questionnaire . . . 6

7. A questionnaire contains the following two questions:

  1. What are the three most important problems in your community today?

    _____

    _____

    _____

  2. People consider different things to be problems in their community. A list of 10 things that some people consider problems follows. Please rank order the list from 1 to 10, where 1 represents the problem <u>you</u> consider <u>most</u> important in your community and 10 represents the problem <u>you</u> consider <u>least</u> important in your community.

Problem	Rank Order
Street cleaning	_____
Corrupt officials	_____
Burglary and other crimes	_____
Mail delivery	_____
Telephone service	_____
Garbage and trash pickup	_____
Inadequate libraries	_____
Lack of up-to-date fire equipment . . .	_____
Low water pressure	_____
Public schools	_____
Other	_____
SPECIFY: _____	

Would a self-administered questionnaire be appropriate for this study, and if so, which <u>type</u> of self-administered questionnaire would you recommend using?

One-to-one self-administered questionnaire 1
Questionnaires administered at various group
    meetings 2
Semisupervised questionnaire passed out as
    people come into community meetings 3
Semisupervised questionnaire passed out as
    people leave various community meetings . . . 4
Questionnaire mailed to county residents' homes . 5
Do not use a self-administered questionnaire 6

8. A study to be administered to high school juniors includes the following questions:

1. Please give me the names of your five closest friends.

_____

_____

_____

_____

_____

2. For *each* person you named in Question 1, please tell whether that person is a male or female, how old, and whether s/he goes to this school.

PERSON #	SEX	AGE	SAME SCHOOL?

3. Have any of these five people ever done anything illegal, like drink or take drugs or steal something?

        No . . . . SKIP TO Q4 1
        Yes . . . . ANSWER A   2

   A. Which of these five people have done something illegal?

_____

   B. What did s/he do?

_____

Would a self-administered questionnaire be appropriate for this study, and if so, which <u>type</u> of self-administered questionnaire would you recommend using?

One-to-one self-administered questionnaire 1
Questionnaires administered in classrooms 2
Semisupervised questionnaire passed out as
    adolescents come to school 3
Semisupervised questionnaire passed out as
    adolescents leave school 4
Questionnaire mailed to students' homes 5
Do not use a self-administered questionnaire 6

9. Identify whether or not a mail questionnaire would be a reasonable way to collect data in the following situations.

a. The City Council wants to find out whether members of the Chamber of Commerce think a new parking structure should be built in the downtown area and the extent to which members would be willing to vote to pay higher taxes to construct it.

b. The school board wants to find out why the number of high school dropouts has increased over the past 5 years.

c. A health insurance company wants to find out how many childhood immunizations its members have had and when they had them.

d. A college sorority wants to find out the current employment status of its alumni.

e. The local newspaper published an article that suggested that county residents will not buy brown eggs. A local grocery store has recently placed an order for brown eggs because it can purchase them at a substantially lower price. After reading the article, the management becomes concerned that the store will lose business if they go ahead with their purchase of brown eggs.

10. Identify why the following questions would or would not work
    well in a self-administered questionnaire.

   a. How much water do you drink every day?

1 ounce	1
2 ounces	2
3 ounces	3
4 ounces	4
5 ounces	5
6 ounces	6
7 ounces	7
8 ounces	8
9 ounces	9
10 ounces	10
11 ounces	11
12 ounces	12
13 ounces	13
14 ounces	14

   b. Please describe all the jobs you have had for pay since
    you were 16 years old.

      _____

      _____

      _____

   c. How many times have you been hospitalized overnight?

Never	GO TO Q53	1
Once	GO TO Q40	2
Twice	GO TO Q27	3
Three or more		
times	CONTINUE	4

d. Do you rent or own your place of residence?

Own 1
Rent 2
Other 3
     SPECIFY: _____

e. What is your current marital status? Are you:

Married 1
Divorced 2
Separated 3
Widowed, or 4
Have you never been married? 5

f. How often do you see or hear from your children or grandchildren?

_____
_____
_____

g. When do you watch the most TV? Would you say:

    Monday 1
    Tuesday 2
    Wednesday 3
    Thursday 4
    Friday 5
    Saturday, or 6
    Sunday 7

h. Have you ever been audited by the IRS?

    Yes 1
    No 2

11. The State Department of Parks and Recreation wants to find out how residents of the state spend their leisure time. What steps should the department take in developing a questionnaire to survey residents?

12. Would the following set of questions make a good self-administered questionnaire? Why or why not?

   1. How often do you vote? Would you say:

      Every election, or 1
      Something else? 2
      SPECIFY: _____

   2. Do you drink milk every day?

      Yes 1
      No 2

   3. What is your highest degree?

      No degree 1
      High school diploma 2
      College degree 3
      Postcollege degree 4
      Something else 5
      SPECIFY: _____

   4. Do you usually vote:

      Republican 1
      Democrat, or 2
      Something else? 3

   5. Are you on a special diet?

      Yes 1
      No 2

6. Are you registered to vote?

        Yes 1
        No 2

7. How many years of schooling have you completed and received credit for?

        Less than 8 years . . . 1
        9-11 years 2
        12 years 3
        More than 12 years . . 4

13. Two companies are considering starting a car pool program. Management has developed the following questionnaire. What kind of instructions will be needed, and where would you put them?

1. How did you get to work yesterday? Did you:

        Drive alone in a car 1
        Drive in a car pool 2
        Take the bus 3
        Ride a motorcycle 4
        Ride a bicycle 5
        Walk, or 6
        Something else? 7
           SPECIFY: _____

2. Was yesterday a typical day for you? Is that the way you usually get to work?

        Yes . . . . . SKIP TO Q3 1
        No . . . . . . ANSWER A 2

A. How do you usually get to work?

Drive alone in a car 1
Drive in a car pool 2
Take the bus 3
Ride a motorcycle 4
Ride a bicycle 5
Walk 6
Something else 7
　　SPECIFY: _____

3. Have you ever used the bus or other public transportation to get to work?

Yes, use public transportation now 1
Yes, used public transportation in the past . . . 2
No, have never used public transportation . . . 3

4. Have you ever considered using public transportation to get to work?

Yes, and currently use it 1
Yes, but decided it was too expensive 2
Yes, but decided it was too inconvenient 3
Yes, but decided against it for some other
　　reason 4
　　SPECIFY: _____
No, never considered using it 5

5. Have you ever used car pools to get to work?

Yes, use a car pool now 1
Yes, used a car pool in the past 2
No, have never used a car pool 3

6. Have you ever considered using a car pool to get to work?

Yes, and currently use it 1
Yes, but decided it was too expensive 2
Yes, but decided it was too inconvenient 3
Yes, but decided against it for some other
    reason 4
    SPECIFY: _____
No, never considered using it 5

7. If the company started a car pool program, would you be interested in using it?

Yes 1
No 2

8. Which of the following incentives would encourage you to enroll in a car pool program?

CIRCLE ALL
THAT APPLY

Reduced fees for car pool parking 1
How long it took to get to work 2
How close to my house it came 3
How frequently it went 4
Extra time off for employees who used it 5
Other 6
    SPECIFY: _____

9. What is your job title?

_____

_____

10. What days of the week do you work?

CIRCLE ALL
THAT APPLY

Monday 1
Tuesday 2
Wednesday 3
Thursday 4
Friday 5
Saturday 6
Sunday 7

11. What time do you come to work?

_____
RECORD TIME COME TO WORK

12. What time do you leave work?

_____
RECORD TIME LEAVE WORK

13. How many miles do you live from work?

_____
RECORD MILES FROM WORK

14. What city or neighborhood do you live in?

_____
RECORD CITY/NEIGHBORHOOD

	Strongly Agree	Agree	Disagree	Strongly Disagree
15. Having people share transportation is a very good idea........	1.....	2.....	3	4
16. The problem of air pollution is overrated...	1.....	2.....	3	4
17. Public transportation is a bigger cause of air pollution than cars..	1.....	2.....	3	4
18. With the right incentives anyone will support car pooling....	1.....	2.....	3	4

19. What is your current marital status? Are you:

Married 1
Divorced 2
Separated 3
Widowed, or 4
Have you never been married? 5

20. Do you have children under 12 living with you?

Yes 1
No 2

21. Are you responsible for taking those children somewhere in the morning or picking them up in the evening?

CIRCLE ALL
THAT APPLY

Yes, taking them in the morning 1
Yes, picking them up in the evening 2
No, not responsible for children 3
No, have no children under 12 4
Other 5
SPECIFY: _____

14. A local health food store wants to find out about the lifestyles of community residents. The owners design the following questionnaire. What suggestions would you make to the owners?

We have designed the following questionnaire to find out about your healthy lifestyle. It will only take you three minutes to fill out and you will feel much better when you realize how healthy your lifestyle is!

1. Of course you exercise every day don't you?   Yes.....1 No.....2

2. When you exercise do you drink a lot of water? Yes, I drink a lot of water and then I run three miles.....1 Yes, I drink some water and run four miles.....2 Sometimes I drink some water before I run.....3 When I run I drink water but when I walk I don't.....4

3. How much do you *avoid* red meat? A lot_____ Some_____ Occasionally_____ When I think of it_____

4. How many people live in your household? Is it just you and one other person or are there more people there?

   Only me. 1

   Me plus one person 2

   Something else 3
   Who else is there?_____

5. When you finished school did you have a high school degree and a college degree or something else?

   High school degree and college degree 1
   Something else 2

6. *Rank order the following list of things that make for a healthy lifestyle from 1 to 10.*

List	Rank
Eating right	_____
Running at least 10 miles a week	_____
Doing meditation	_____
Getting 8 hours of sleep every night	_____
Eating leafy green vegetables every day	_____
Avoiding situations that make you angry	_____
Avoiding caffeine	_____
Never eating sugar	_____
Thinking good thoughts	_____
Lifting weights	_____

15. What kinds of specifications need to be written for the questionnaire included in Question 12?

16. What resources would you pursue if you were looking for a source for the following types of samples? What are the advantages and disadvantages of each source?

    a. A sample of residences in your local community?

    b. A sample of lawyers in your community?

    c. A national sample of physicians?

    d. A sample of local high school students?

17. You are the Director of Nursing Services at your local county hospital. You are responsible for a nursing staff of 300. You are contemplating a change in shift hours and want to know how your staff would react to this change. There are 10 service divisions within the department and two shifts on each service, with approximately 15 nurses per service per shift. You have decided that a survey of 100 nurses would be ample to determine what the overall reaction of the nursing staff would be. How would you select a sample, and what means of data collection would you use?

18. a. What are the components of a group self-administered study?

    b. What are the components of a mailed survey?

19. You are conducting a mailed survey of recipients of Aid to Families with Dependent Children (AFDC) who completed a job training program run by your department last year. You have mailed to 300 individuals who completed their training and have received only 50 completed returns. You have decide to select another 300 names to send the questionnaire to in order to increase the number of responses. Is this appropriate?

20. Make a list of standard sample tracking procedures.

21. From your mailed survey, the following envelopes have been returned by the Postal Service with the following reason for nondelivery. How would you go about trying to readdress them?

    a. Address: John Crawford
                           1418 Ork Street
                           Tree Town, OH 76024

       Reason for return: No such street

    b. Address: Mrs. Robert Adams
                           907 River Ave. Apt. #
                           Redbank, N.J. 85072

       Reason for return: Undeliverable as addressed

    c. Address: Julius Rosen
                           247 B3 First Ave.
                           New Bedford, MA 456023

       Reason for return: No such number

    d. Address: Doris Newhouse
                           5201 Orange Grove Ave.
                           Orange, CA 91204

       Reason for return: Not in this ZIP code

ANSWERS

1. Option 4:   The population should be sufficiently literate that they can respond to a mail questionnaire and the company should have sufficient money to send out a mail questionnaire. Respondents would also probably be more honest if they completed the questionnaires outside the workplace.

2. Option 3:   The PTA wants to solicit the support and participation of active members. Active members are more likely to come to meetings and they are more likely to be interested in enhancing the school's resources. Passing out questionnaires as members come into a meeting increases the likelihood that they will be completed during the meeting and returned at the end.

3. Option 5:   The fact that the group of interest is elderly and composed of recent immigrants who probably speak Russian rather than English argues against the use of a self-administered questionnaire and for the use of telephone or face-to-face interviews.

4. Options 1, 2, or 3:   The procedure used to test this questionnaire would vary with the amount of resources the clinic has available to develop the questionnaire and the extent to which it thinks that the questionnaire as drafted is incomplete or unclear. One-to-one self-administered questionnaires would allow the clinic to explore patients' responses in the most detail but would make it difficult to administer the questionnaire to large numbers of patients in a short period of time. Group administrations where patients were encouraged to discuss the questionnaire would probably provide more information than semisupervised questionnaires. Both techniques would allow for relatively rapid feedback on the questionnaire.

5. Option 4:   Questionnaires passed out as workers left the factory would probably provide a fairly representative and rapid assessment of the situation and allow the surveyor an opportunity for answering questions and encouraging returns. Questionnaires administered in groups at work or distributed as workers come in to work would increase the response rate but also probably increase the likelihood that workers would talk about the questionnaire and that the "squeaky wheels" would have undue influence over the responses. In general, factory workers are not going to respond at high rates to a mail questionnaire.

6. Option 5:   The board has sufficient money and the addresses needed to conduct a mail questionnaire but *not* enough money to conduct telephone interviews with 500 people. Although responses will probably be biased toward those with more education, the amount of money available would allow for a substantial amount of follow-up by mail and even by telephone. The responses to a mail questionnaire would be substantially more representative of the county population than would questionnaires distributed at various community meetings.

7. Option 6:   Two things argue against using a self-administered questionnaire for this study. First, an open-ended question is followed by a closed-ended question that contains a list of problems. In an interview, respondents will not have that list available when they are asked Question 1, but in a self-administered questionnaire they will. As a result, they are likely to select items from the list in responding to Question 1. Second, the list included in Question 2 is long, and respondents are asked to rank order it. This is a difficult task for respondents to do without assistance from an interviewer and argues against the inclusion of such a question in a self- administered questionnaire.

8. Option 6: This questionnaire has too many open-ended questions and is too complicated to expect students to complete by themselves. It is also subject to misreporting and bias if administered in a school setting, and parents are likely to insist on looking at the questionnaire if it is mailed to students' homes. Special procedures have to be followed when people under the age of 18 are used in *any* kind of research study. Generally, this involves obtaining permission from both the parent or guardian and the adolescent. Finally, this is not a very clearly written set of questions *even for* an interview.

9. a. Yes. The Chamber of Commerce is an identifiable group that should be motivated to respond and capable of responding to a mail questionnaire.

    b. No. It may take some exploratory work to find out how best to conduct this study. Furthermore, up-to-date lists and addresses are unlikely to exist for students who dropped out prior to the current year, and we cannot assume that dropouts would be either motivated to respond or capable of responding to a mail questionnaire.

    c. No. Data on childhood immunizations is difficult to get under any circumstances. It requires that people *either* have records *or* a parent available that can provide a complete listing of the type of immunizations they had as children and the dates of those immunizations. It is unlikely that respondents would be able to provide such information in response to a mail questionnaire.

    d. Yes. Sorority members can be expected to identify with the organization and be motivated to respond to its requests. Furthermore, the topic of the study is current and restricted.

    e. No. The management does not have a list of persons who regularly patronize their grocery store. They would be better advised to interview persons who come into the store over the period of a typical week to find out (a) how they feel about brown eggs, (b) whether they read the newspaper article, and (c) how regularly they buy groceries at this particular store.

10. a. No. The question is better than the response categories in that it is short and precise. It does contain an assumption that respondents drink the same amount of water every day. The answer categories are ridiculous. First, many people probably do not know what an "ounce" represents in volume. It is better to ask them about "typical cups" or "typical glasses" of water while simultaneously defining the number of ounces in a typical cup (6 ounces) or a typical glass (8 ounces). Second, the range of answers, while mutually exclusive, is *not* exhaustive; it does not allow for people who drink no water or those who drink more than 14 ounces. Third, the list of responses is unnecessarily long and skewed toward lesser amounts of water.

b. No. This is a burdensome question for a respondent to answer validly without assistance from an interviewer. First, it is open-ended. Second, it asks older respondents in particular to provide a great deal of historical information without providing any guidance as to the *order* in which information should be provided or the *amount* of information that should be provided about each job.

c. No. The question itself is all right, but the complicated skip pattern set up in the response alternatives argues against a self-administered questionnaire.

d. Yes. This question is short and specific and the response categories are exhaustive and mutually exclusive. Furthermore, the residual other is unlikely to generate many responses but ensures that respondents who do not feel that the other two answers represent them can express themselves.

e. Yes. This question is short and specific, and the response categories are mutually exclusive and exhaustive if we are interested in finding out about respondents' legal marital status. In some populations, the surveyor might want to add a second question that asked about unmarried co-habitation of either same-sex or different-sex couples.

f. No. This is even more than a double-barreled question! Also, it is open ended.

g. No. As written, the response categories are not exhaustive; they do not provide for respondents who watch no television or for those who watch equal amounts of television on multiple days. In the question itself, it would be better to say "television" instead of "TV." Although most persons probably understand the abbreviation, better safe than sorry!

h. No. The response categories are fine, and the question is short and precise, but it contains abstract terms (e.g., audited) and jargon (e.g., IRS) that may not be understood by some respondents.

11. The State Department of Parks and Recreation should (a) conduct a literature review to see what, if anything, has been published about leisure time; (b) consider adopting or adapting questionnaires developed by others; and (c) pretest one or more draft questionnaires to make sure that the questionnaire is understandable to a representative sample of the state's residents and to estimate the cost of conducting the survey. After pretesting, the department may find that it cannot obtain reliable and valid information through a mail questionnaire.

12. No, not as written. The questions are not logically ordered. Within any given topic, questions are not ordered from less complex to more complex. For example, respondents are asked if they vote before they are asked if they are registered. Question 3 is unlikely to be understood where it is and should be preceded by Question 7. There are no instructions to the respondent, nor are there any transitions between questions or topics. Question 1 was written by a lazy surveyor and is likely to result in many different answers in the "residual other" category that will have to be postcoded.

13. As written, this questionnaire needs four kinds of instructions. First, general instructions need to be provided and a decision made regarding whether these general instructions will be in a cover letter or on the first page of the questionnaire. The selection of procedure will probably vary with how management plans to administer the questionnaire. If the plan is to distribute it at the workplace or as employees come to or leave the workplace, instructions could be put on the questionnaire itself. If the plan is to send the questionnaire to employees' homes, a cover letter should be used. These general instructions need to explain the purpose of the questionnaire and who is conducting the study, describe how confidentiality will be protected, explain how respondents were chosen, provide motivation for employees to respond to the questionnaire, anticipate any problems or concerns that employees might have in responding to the questionnaire, provide a way for employees to get more information about the study or confirm its legitimacy, and tell employees how to return the completed questionnaire. If a cover letter is used, it should be printed on letterhead and, if possible, a personal salutation added.

Second, brief sets of instructions need to be provided before Question 1, between Questions 8 and 9, and before Question 19. These instructions "alert" respondents to the upcoming topic and to transitions between topics.

Third, detailed instructions need to be provided before Question 15 that explain to the respondent that these are questions about opinions or attitudes, that there are no right or wrong answers, and how to use the available answer categories.

Finally, an ending needs to be provided for the questionnaire that (a) encourages respondents to comment on the questionnaire or add additional information, (b) thanks respondents, and (c) repeats what the employee is supposed to do with the completed questionnaire.

14. This questionnaire breaks almost every rule of questionnaire construction. First, the print is too small. Second, italics are used, which are difficult to read. Third, the owners of the

health food store clearly have an "agenda." Their questions do not allow for the possibility that respondents might *not* do the things that the owners consider healthy. Fourth, the responses for Question 3 are all vague qualifiers. Fifth, there is no consistency in spacing or formatting. Some response categories are listed vertically while others are listed horizontally. Et cetera, et cetera.

15. Specifications should document the purpose of the study, how respondents were selected to participate, how the questionnaires were administered, the number and timing of follow-up contacts, and *why* each question or set of questions was included in the questionnaire. If questions were adopted or adapted from other studies, the source of those questions, the reason for their selection, and the reason for any changes should be explained.

16. a. SOURCE: The most ideal situation would be to have a 100% list of all residences in your sampled community. Short of going out and hand-listing every address on every street in the area, you will probably have to resort to less reliable resources. Check commercial mailing houses, which are the companies that mail fliers, ads, product samples, and the like to households in the area. Speak to the local telephone company to determine the rate of unlisted residential telephones in your study area. If the unlisted rate is low, the telephone directory may be an adequate resource. Also, check with the main depot of your local Postal Service, which may be able to recommend a source for addresses.

   ADVANTAGES: Commercial sources usually provide quick, economical access to large numbers of addresses. Often, these resources will be able to provide many of the services required in a survey mailing. They most likely will have computerized lists and therefore will be able to pull a sample according to your sampling specifications, run your address labels for you, fold and stuff your survey materials mechanically, and mechanically post your mailing.

DISADVANTAGES: Using commercial sources such as mail order companies and postal addressing firms probably does not include more casual residences, such as garages converted to living space, unless these changes have been made according to local code and legally registered on the local housing rosters as a residential address. Telephone directories may have high household coverage; however, there will still be those residences with unlisted numbers that will be missed. Also, there may be a considerable number of listings where the address is suppressed. It is also unknown if one telephone covers more than one residence or if one residence has more than one telephone number and therefore has more than one chance of being included in the sample.

b. SOURCE: The commercial listings or "Yellow Pages" section of your local telephone directory is probably as good a resource as any. The State Bar Association would be another good source, but it may limit access to its files.

ADVANTAGES: The local telephone directory is an easily available and inexpensive resource. The State Bar Association would most likely have the names and addresses computerized so that accessing and producing a mailing sample would be considerably more time efficient and possibly cost efficient.

DISADVANTAGES: The local telephone directories will miss any lawyer or law group that has not paid for listing in the commercial pages, so there is the probability that you will miss some individuals in your sample. In the case of law firms, it may be difficult getting the name of each individual lawyer working within the firm. The State Bar Association may not have current addresses for all individuals.

c. SOURCE: Most practicing physicians are members of the American Medical Association (AMA). You can contact them to explore the possibility of obtaining a sample of physicians from them. If a sample is not available from the AMA, there are commercial companies that maintain lists of professionals such as physicians to sell to firms, say, pharmaceutical companies.

ADVANTAGES: Both resources will have computerized files, making it easy to select a sample and produce mailing labels.

DISADVANTAGES: Getting in touch with an appropriate and cooperative individual in the AMA may require extra effort. Neither resource is free. Neither resource will have 100% coverage, but the AMA probably has a more complete listing of practicing physicians. Both lists will not be 100% up-to-date on current addresses. Getting the names of individuals in group practices or health maintenance organizations (HMOs) may be a problem.

d. SOURCE: Contact the administrative offices of your local school district for public schools and individual administrative offices for private schools. You will have to obtain permission "systemwide" to be able to access any information. Once you have obtained this access, you will have to contact the high schools you have selected for inclusion in your sample. Schools may place different conditions upon your accessing students. If you are not taking a 100% sample in the classroom, an identification number may have to be used for sampling rather than a name because you may not be given access to individual names. You may be asked to distribute a letter requesting signed permission from a parent or guardian of each student to have him or her participate in your study. This will probably have to be coordinated through a "homeroom" teacher. If and when parental consent is obtained, you will probably have to also have consent from each student. If you are not allowed address access to students you may have to either arrange for group administration of your survey at some time when all students are in one place, like "homeroom" or assembly, or supply the student with a packet to be completed at some later time and either mailed back or returned to a designated location at the school.

If access is denied by the school board, you may have to resort to using a "convenience" sample by going to places in your community where high school students are accessible, such as church groups, fast food outlets, or other such attractions. You may find a situation where you can conduct a group administration or at least hand out forms to be completed at another time and returned by mail.

ADVANTAGES: A school-based sample of students essentially guarantees you that nearly every student in your area has the possibility of being selected. The group setting allows for group administration or distribution, maximizing the number of individuals you can survey in one contact. Although the time spent obtaining access may be considerable, there is virtually no cost in obtaining the sample.

Convenience samples are generally easy to access. The cost to obtain the sample is minimal. Data can be collected in a very short period of time.

DISADVANTAGES: School-based samples are fine if all you want to represent are students. If you are interested in representing teenagers, you will miss that portion of the population that has dropped out of school. If you use a school-based sample, any student who is not present at school on the day of your administration or distribution will not have an opportunity to participate in the study. Therefore, your sample has less chance of being truly representative.

Convenience samples can be extremely biased. The resource from which you obtain your sample will usually limit the representativeness of the sample. For example, if you go to video arcades, you will find only those students who go to these types of amusements. The return on this type of sample may be extremely low. There is little incentive for the student to comply with participation unless the topic is of overwhelming interest.

17. Each service/shift should be sampled for 5 respondents. 15 ÷ 5 = 3. Make an alphabetical list by service by shift of all nurses on the staff. Take every third name. To avoid possible influence from co-workers and to protect respondent anonymity, you would probably mail the questionnaire to the nurses at their home addresses and provide stamped, self-addressed envelopes for the return.

18. a. Group Administration Packet Checklist

   ✓ Sample
     Access? Means of selection

   ✓ Schedule
     Calendar of date/time/place

   ✓ Informed consent
     If necessary. Quantity?

   ✓ Cover letter
     Print quantity?

   ✓ Questionnaire
     Print quantity?

   ✓ Incentive (if used)
     Quantity?

   ✓ Other handouts (if any)
     Quantity?

   ✓ Means of retrieval
     Collect/box/mailback?

   b. Mailing Packet Checklist

   ✓ Sample labels/addresses
     Quantity?

   ✓ Outgoing mail envelopes
     Sample size?

✓ Size of questionnaire?
  Additional materials?

✓ Outgoing postage
  Metered or stamped?

✓ Cover letter
  Print quantity?

✓ Questionnaire
  Print quantity?

✓ Incentive (if used)
  Quantity?

✓ Other inserts (if any)
  Quantity?

✓ Return mail envelope
  Postage-paid business reply/metered/stamps?

19. No. By not using a follow-up to increase response rates from the original sample nor tracking bad addresses, you may be missing important feedback about the success of your program. For example, the program may have been highly successful, and a significant number of individuals have obtained good jobs and moved on and are no longer at their original addresses. Conversely, the program may have had very little impact on most of the respondents' lives, and they are not motivated to respond. By replacement sampling you will probably never receive responses from either of these types of participants, and you will not have accurate information with which to evaluate your program.

20. SAMPLE TRACKING PROCEDURES GUIDELINE

   ✓ Check for typographical or clerical errors in address

   ✓ Remail new packet to each corrected address

   ✓ Stamp outgoing envelopes "ADDRESS CORRECTION REQUESTED" and correct address file based on corrected returns

✓ Remail to corrected addresses

✓ Check with sample provider for updates (if applicable)

✓ Check telephone directories, telephone directory information, and reverse directories

✓ Check utilities/Department of Motor Vehicles

21. a. If you have checked with your sample source and the results are the same, there is probably a typographical error in the street name. "Ork" would be a fairly unusual name for a street. Look for a likely name spelled similarly, such as "Oak." If Oak Street DOES exist in the sampled area, try readdressing it to that address.

   b. Check with your sample source for the missing apartment number. If the result is the same, try to determine the correct apartment number through the appropriate telephone directory. If the name is listed with a telephone number, you can try calling the number, explaining your purpose, and asking for the correct address. If the building is accessible to you, you might look at mailboxes or the building directory to see if you can determine the apartment number. If the number cannot be found, try leaving "Apt. #" out of the address entirely and see if the postal person might know the name and deliver it without the apartment number on the address.

   c. In this case, the apartment number appears to be a part of the street address. Never type the unit number next to the street address. Rather, put it after the street name or on the next line.

   d. The wrong ZIP code was used on this address. There are often ZIP code directories available at main branches of public libraries, or you can call the post office and ask for the ZIP code that covers that address. In this case, the ZIP code was one number off on the final number of the code. It should have read 91203. It is sometimes the case that a ZIP code will change numbers in the middle of a street.

Suggested Readings

Aday, L. A. (1989). *Designing and conducting health surveys.* San Francisco: Jossey-Bass.

Basic textbook on the design and administration of all kinds of surveys. Draws on methodological work on surveys in general and health surveys in particular.

Aquilino, W. S. (1994). Interview mode effects in surveys of drug and alcohol use. *Public Opinion Quarterly, 58,* 210-240.

Reports the results of a field experiment designed to study respondents' willingness to admit use of illicit drugs and alcohol in three conditions: personal interviews that incorporated the use of a self-administered questionnaire to obtain the sensitive information, personal interviews without a self-administered questionnaire, and telephone interviews. The use of a self-administered questionnaire within a personal interview resulted in somewhat higher estimates of illicit substance use, and telephone interviews resulted in somewhat lower estimates.

Berry, S. H., & Kanouse, D. E. (1987). Physician response to a mailed survey: An experiment in timing of payment. *Public Opinion Quarterly, 51,* 102-114.

Compares the response rates of questionnaires mailed to physicians when $20 was included in the original mailing with those promised $20 upon receipt of the completed questionnaire. Prepayment was found to have significant positive effects on response rates.

Bourque, L. B., & Clark, V. A. (1992). *Processing data: The survey example.* Newbury Park, CA: Sage.

Systematic explanation of how to perform data processing using today's technology. The authors adopt a broad definition of data processing that starts with selecting a data collection strategy and ends when data transformations are complete. Much of the material covered has direct applicability to the design, administration, and processing of self-administered questionnaires.

Bourque, L. B., Cosand, B. B., Drews, C., Waring, G. O., Lynn, M., Cartwright, C., & PERK Study Group. (1986). Reported satisfaction, fluctuation of vision, and glare among patients one year after surgery in the Prospective Evaluation of Radial Keratotomy (PERK) Study. *Archives of Ophthalmology, 104,* 356-363.

Provides a description of the PERK Study population and how results of the surgery related to satisfaction and side effects 1 year after surgery on the first eye.

Bourque, L. B., Lynn, M. J., Waring, G. O., Cartwright, C., & PERK Study Group. (1994). Spectacle and contact lens wearing six years after radial keratotomy in the Prospective Evaluation of Radial Keratotomy Study. *Ophthalmology, 101,* 421-431.

Describes the PERK study population 6 years after surgery on the first eye and 5 years after surgery on the second eye. The questionnaire used in this study provided the basis for the questionnaire discussed in the examples in this book.

Bradburn, N. M. (1983). Response effects. In P. H. Rossi, J. D. Wright, & A. B. Anderson (Eds.), *Handbook of survey research* (pp. 289-328). New York: Academic Press.

Focuses primarily on questionnaires used in interviews. However, information presented on open versus closed questions, question order, question length and wording, and retrospective memory have relevance for the design of all questionnaires—including self-administered ones.

Brook, R. H., Ware, J. E., Rogers, W. H., Keeler, E. B., Davies, A. R., Donald, C. A., Goldberg, G. A., Lohr, K. N., Masthay, P. C., & Newhouse, J. P. (1983). Does free care improve adults' health? Results from a randomized controlled trial. *New England Journal of Medicine, 309*, 1426-1434.

One of the first major publications that reported the results of RAND's Health Insurance Experiment. Includes a description of the design of the study and the data collection techniques used.

California WIC Program manual (WIC No. 210-60). (1994). Washington, DC: Department of Health, Education, and Welfare (overseer of state programs).

Source of the information reported in Chapter 2 on the federal Women, Infants and Children (WIC) Program, which is administered at the state level.

Church, A. H. (1993). Estimating the effect of incentives on mail survey response rates: A meta-analysis. *Public Opinion Quarterly, 57*, 62-79.

Reports the results of a meta-analysis of 38 experimental and quasi-experimental studies that implemented some form of incentive so as to increase response rates in a mail survey. The use of prepaid monetary or nonmonetary rewards included with the initial mailing were compared with the use of monetary or nonmonetary rewards provided conditional upon return of the questionnaire. The effects of incentives were found to be modest, with those that included rewards in the initial mailing being more effective in increasing response rates.

Converse, J. M., & Presser, S. (1986). *Survey questions: Handcrafting the standardized questionnaire.* Newbury Park, CA: Sage.

Succinct overview of what is involved in designing question-naires, with particular attention to questionnaires administered in interviews and studies that focus on attitudes and opinions. Much of the information provided has relevance, however, to self-administered questionnaires.

Council of Professional Associations on Federal Statistics. (1993). *Providing incentives to survey respondents: Final report.* Washington, DC: General Services Administration, Regulatory Information Service Center.

Newsletter dealing with statistical gathering and matters of confidentiality.

Dillman, D. A. (1978). *Mail and telephone surveys: The total design method.* New York: John Wiley.

Classic reference on the design of mail questionnaires. A "must" for those interested in developing expertise in this area.

Fink, A., & Kosecoff, J. (1985). *How to conduct surveys: A step-by-step guide.* Beverly Hills, CA: Sage.

A "how to" book good for both the novice and more experienced surveyor. Purpose, goals, and examples are realistic.

Fowler, F. J., Jr. (1993). *Survey research methods* (2nd ed.). Newbury Park, CA: Sage.

A comprehensive summary of the methods of survey research and the sources of error inherent in each. Provides a guide for calculating survey statistics and error measurement.

Fox, R. J., Crask, M. R., & Kim, J. (1988). Mail survey response rate: A meta-analysis of selected techniques for inducing response. *Public Opinion Quarterly, 52,* 467-491.

Reports the results of a meta-analysis of the experimental studies that have examined 10 different factors felt to influence response rates to mail surveys. Results indicate that such things as advance letters, sponsorship, color of paper, the type of postage used, and follow-ups increase response rates. Increases in the amount of a monetary incentive appear to have decreasing marginal gains on response rates.

Henry, G. T. (1990). *Practical sampling.* Newbury Park, CA: Sage.

A sampling textbook designed for the "common surveyor." Not overly technical but highly practical.

James, M. J., & Bolstein, R. (1990). The effect of monetary incentives and follow-up mailings on the response rate and response quality in mail surveys. *Public Opinion Quarterly, 54,* 346-361.

The separate and joint effect of monetary incentives and follow-up mailings were compared in increasing response rates. Four mailings without an incentive produced a higher response rate than a single mailing with an incentive, but a combination of follow-up mailings and a higher monetary incentive produced higher response rates than follow-up mailings without an incentive. There was, however, some evidence of response bias across the different treatment groups.

Jobe, J. B., & Loftus, E. F. (Eds.). (1991). Cognition and survey measurement [Special issue]. *Applied Cognitive Psychology, 5*(3).

The collaboration to which this issue is devoted represents a movement to blend, or merge, the scientific value embedded in both the laboratory and naturalistic research settings and to do this under conditions that make possible the emergence of a methodologically innovative, mutually supportive interdiscipline.

Kalton, G. (1983). *Introduction to survey sampling.* Beverly Hills, CA: Sage.

A good primer on sampling theory for the beginning surveyor. Provides good illustrations, practical considerations, and problems likely to be encountered in sampling.

Kraemer, H. C., & Thiemann, S. (1987). *How many subjects? Statistical power analysis in research.* Newbury Park, CA: Sage.

Introduces a simple technique of statistical power analysis to compute approximate sample sizes and power for a wide variety of research designs.

Kraus, J. F. (1990). Homicide while at work: Persons, industries, and occupations at high risk. *American Journal of Public Health, 77,* 1285-1312.

Represents one of the articles used in conducting a literature review in preparation for the Workplace Assault Study. A study of work-related homicides in California from 1979 to 1981 reported an average annual rate of 1.5 homicides per 100,000 workers with a male-to-female ratio of 4.2:1. Rates were highest for police (20.8), security guards (16.5), and taxi drivers (19.0) and were elevated for persons who worked at night in retail or service jobs, such as convenience store clerks, bartenders, and janitors.

Kruger, R. A. (1994). *Focus groups: A practical guide for applied research* (2nd ed.). Thousand Oaks, CA: Sage.

Provides a detailed discussion of the focus group technique. Describes characteristics, conditions of use, and implementation.

Krysan, M., Schuman, H., Scott, L. J., & Beatty, P. (1994). Response rates and response content in mail versus face-to-face surveys. *Public Opinion Quarterly, 58,* 381-399.

Compares response rates from an hour-long, face-to-face interview with those from a shorter mail questionnaire. Both surveys were administered in Detroit in 1992. Response rates did not differ for white respondents but were significantly lower for black respondents who received mail questionnaires; responses differed by administrative procedure, with respondents to the mail questionnaire expressing more negative attitudes toward racial integration and affirmative action.

Rasinski, K. A., Mingay, D., & Bradburn, N. M. (1994). Do respondents really "mark all that apply" on self-administered questions? *Public Opinion Quarterly, 58*, 400-408.

Instructions to "mark all that apply" were compared to questions where each of the applicable categories was asked in the form of "yes-no" questions. Fewer response options were selected with the "mark all that apply" format, but whether that means such formats result in underreporting or "yes-no" responses result in overreporting cannot be assessed in this data set.

Schuman, H., & Presser, S. (1981). *Questions and answers in attitude surveys.* San Diego: Academic Press.

Reports the findings from a series of experiments conducted to determine how the way in which questions about attitudes are asked influences the data obtained.

Sheatsley, P. B. (1983). Questionnaire construction and item writing. In P. H. Rossi, J. D. Wright, & A. B. Anderson (Eds.), *Handbook of survey research* (pp. 289-328). New York: Academic Press.

Basic reference on issues to consider in deciding whether questionnaires are an appropriate method for collecting data, the kind of administrative procedure that is appropriately used, and how to develop questions and questionnaires.

Sudman, S., & Bradburn, N. M. (1982). *Asking questions*. San Francisco: Jossey-Bass.

Describes the development of questions used in structured questionnaires or interview schedules used in social and market research. Covers general issues on questionnaire design; the development of questions on nonthreatening and threatening behaviors, attitudes, and demographic characteristics; the development of response categories; and question wording and context.

Tanur, J. (Ed.). (1992). *Questions about questions: Inquiries into the cognitive bases of surveys*. New York: Russell Sage Foundation.

Questions about the rigid standardization imposes on the survey interview receive a thorough airing as the authors show how traditional survey formats violate the usual norms of conversational behavior and potentially endanger the validity of the data collected.

U.S. Bureau of the Census. (1992). *Census of population and housing: 1990, United States. Summary Tape File B* [Computer file]. Washington, DC: U.S. Department of Commerce (producer); Ann Arbor, MI: Interuniversity Consortium for Political and Social Research (distributor).

Source of 1990 Census data reported in Chapter 2.

Ware, J. E., Jr., Snow, K. K., Dosinski, M., & Gandek, B. (1993). *SF-36 Health Survey: Manual and interpretation guide*. Boston: Health Institute, New England Medical Center.

Describes some of the scales developed out of RAND's Health Insurance Experiment and Medical Outcomes Study. Provides information about questions included in the PERK Study.

Washington State Department of Labor and Industries. (1993). *Study of assaults on state employees at eastern and western state hospitals*. Tacoma: Safety and Health Assessment and Research for Prevention.

Represents one of the studies examined in the literature review for the Workplace Assault Study. In a study of two Washington State psychiatric hospitals, questionnaire responses were compared with injuries reported in various official reports. The number of assaults reported was roughly comparable for incident reports and questionnaire responses. However, Workers' Compensation and OSHA logs substantially underestimated the total number of occurrences in a given period. Whereas 12.4 injuries per 100 nursing FTEs (full-time equivalents) were reported in OSHA logs, 21.6 to 28.7 workers' compensation claims were made, 63.4 to 70.9 assaults per 100 FTEs were reported in incident reports, and more than 70% of the ward staff completing questionnaires reported experiencing at least one physical assault leading to mild injury.

Weisberg, H. F., Krosnick, J. A., & Bowen, B. D. (1989). *An introduction to survey research and data analysis* (2nd ed.). Glenview, IL: HarperCollins College Division.

A more sophisticated presentation of survey research methods, with greater focus than most guides on data analysis, report writing, and the evaluation of completed surveys.

Wentland, E. J., & Smith, K. W. (1993). *Survey responses: An evaluation of their validity*. San Diego: Academic Press.

Thirty-seven studies conducted between 1944 and 1988 were included in a meta-analysis that assessed the accuracy of individuals' responses to questionnaires when compared to independent criteria. Discrepancies varied with the extent to which the requested information was accessible to respondents, subject matter, and characteristics of the questionnaire.

Yammarino, F. J., Skinner, S. J., & Childers, T. L. (1991). Understanding mail survey response behavior: A meta-analysis. *Public Opinion Quarterly, 55,* 613-639.

A meta-analysis of studies designed to induce mail survey response rates. Results indicated that repeated contacts in the form of preliminary notification and follow-ups, appeals, inclusion of a return envelope, postage, and monetary incentives effectively increased response rates.

About the Authors

LINDA B. BOURQUE, PhD, is a professor in the Department of Community Health Sciences in the School of Public Health at the University of California at Los Angeles, where she teaches courses in research design and survey methodology. Her research is in the areas of ophthalmic clinical trials and intentional and unintentional injury. She is author or coauthor of 50 scientific articles and the books *Defining Rape* and *Processing Data: The Survey Example* (with Virginia Clark).

EVE P. FIELDER, DrPH, has more than 30 years' experience in survey research. Since her beginnings in market research, she has had working experience in all phases of survey methods and has conducted hundreds of surveys, both commercial and academic. For the past 23 years, she has been with the Institute for Social Science Research at the University of California at Los Angeles, where she is Director of the Survey Research Center, and has taught survey research methods at UCLA and at the University of Southern California. She has consulted on studies for numerous organizations and community service agencies and has a strong background in cross-cultural research.